The Arden Introduction to Reading Shakespeare

RELATED ARDEN SHAKESPEARE TITLES

Essential Shakespeare, Pamela Bickley and Jenny Stevens
Hamlet: Language and Writing, Dympna Callaghan
The Tempest: Language and Writing, Brinda Charry
Shakespeare Up Close, edited by Russ McDonald, Nicholas D. Nace and Travis D. Williams
Macbeth: Language and Writing, Emma Smith

The Arden Introduction to Reading Shakespeare

JEREMY LOPEZ

THE ARDEN SHAKESPEARE
LONDON • NEW YORK • OXFORD • NEW DELHI • SYDNEY

THE ARDEN SHAKESPEARE
Bloomsbury Publishing Plc
50 Bedford Square, London, WC1B 3DP, UK
1385 Broadway, New York, NY 10018, USA

BLOOMSBURY, THE ARDEN SHAKESPEARE and the Arden Shakespeare logo are trademarks of Bloomsbury Publishing Plc

First published in Great Britain 2019

Cover design by Dani Leigh
Cover image © Marc Volk/gettyimages.co.uk

A catalogue record for this book is available from the British Library.

A catalog record for this book is available from the Library of Congress.

ISBN: HB: 978-1-4725-8104-4
PB: 978-1-4725-8102-0
ePDF: 978-1-4725-8105-1
eBook: 978-1-4725-8103-7

Typeset by Integra Software Services Pvt. Ltd.
Printed and bound in Great Britain

CONTENTS

Preface vii
Acknowledgements ix
Note to the Reader x

PART ONE

1 The Title 3
2 Stage Directions 11
3 Scenes 26
4 The Whole Play 41

PART TWO

5 First Words 55
6 The First Act 65
7 The Third Act 72
8 The Second and Fourth Acts 80
9 The Last Act 90
10 Last Words 101

PART THREE

11 Patterned Language 113
12 Characters 124

PART FOUR

13 Metre 141
14 Textual Variation 150

Epilogue 161

Selected Further Reading 163
Index 165

PREFACE

Shakespeare's plays are works of art made out of words. To read the plays closely, that is, to pay careful attention to the multiple, shifting meanings of and relationships between their words, is to gain a deep and lasting appreciation for the complex artistry of their construction and of their effects. This book provides an introduction to the practice of reading Shakespeare's plays closely, and some examples of the interpretive work that such close reading can enable.

Structurally, the book is a guided tour through some of the most productive sites in Shakespeare's plays for close reading and interpretation. Thematically, its overarching concern is with the complex relation between individual parts of a play and the dramatic whole to which they belong. The book is divided into four parts, comprising fourteen chapters. The chapters, all of which are structured identically (three main sections framed by a brief overview and a brief conclusion), state their goals pretty explicitly, so I will describe them only very briefly here. The four chapters of Part One deal with starting-points, that is, the play's title and stage directions, which are among the first things a reader encounters in a play; with the scene, which, I argue, is for Shakespeare the fundamental unit of dramatic construction; and with the entire play, which, I suggest, you ought to read quickly and without worrying too much about understanding it all, before you begin the work of close reading in earnest. Part Two is concerned with dramatic structure: in six chapters, it moves from the first words of a play to the last, taking the act as its primary unit of analysis. Part Three establishes two large categories for analysis, patterned language and characters, and draws on many of the close-reading methods and techniques modelled in the preceding ten chapters. Part Four focuses on two rather technical matters that must inform any really thorough close reading: metre (with specific reference to Shakespeare's sonnets) and textual variation. Finally, there is a short Epilogue, in which I reflect briefly on the book's methods and goals, followed by a list of suggestions for further reading.

The close-reading methods modelled in this book will be useful to inexperienced readers of Shakespeare, and even experienced readers should find readings here that are new, interesting and productive. But the book should not be mistaken for, or used as, a course in Shakespeare studies. I provide little information about the theatre, society or politics of Shakespeare's time. I do not discuss the Shakespearean performance tradition in any detail, and I engage only briefly with matters of textual history. My discussion of metre is deliberately non-technical. And although I refer to almost every play in the canon at least once, I have not made any attempt to distribute my examples evenly, or to key them to the chronology of Shakespeare's career; indeed, you will find that I tend to return to a handful of plays (*Romeo and Juliet, A Midsummer Night's Dream, 1 Henry IV, Othello, Richard II, The Comedy of Errors, All's Well That Ends Well* and *Titus Andronicus*) with particular frequency. Furthermore, my close readings do not gesture outward to the political and ethical questions and interpretations that you are likely to encounter in most classroom discussions and scholarly writing about Shakespeare. Rather, they tend to turn inward to the main subject of this book: the complex experience of reading or watching a Shakespeare play, word by word, line by line, scene by scene and act by act. This inward focus is not meant to suggest that Shakespeare's plays should, or even can, be read outside of their (or our) historical context. Rather, it is meant to allow the book to fulfil, as efficiently as possible, its particular mandate: to provide readers who are new to studying Shakespeare with some places to start, and with a spur to further reading. This book will probably be most useful in conjunction with a course or other reading you are already doing on Shakespeare; its focused approach should help you cultivate habits of attention that will support any interpretive approach to the plays that you decide to pursue.

ACKNOWLEDGEMENTS

This book has taken a long time to complete, mostly because it has been read carefully by colleagues who were not shy about pointing out its shortcomings: Bill Carroll, Chris Warley and two anonymous readers for Bloomsbury Publishing. One of these anonymous readers was particularly thorough, perceptive and uncompromising in his or her assessment of multiple drafts; this reader repeatedly saved me from my own worst habits, and improved both my readings and my writing. The book is much stronger for all the criticism it has received. Needless to say, any errors and absurdities that remain are entirely my responsibility.

Six different groups of students taking the English 220Y Shakespeare course at the University of Toronto were subjected to many of the close readings discussed in this book as I developed them; answering these students' questions, reading their essays and talking to them in office hours did much to help me refine my methods and arguments. My research assistants Divna Stojanovic and Jonathan Dick provided invaluable assistance at various stages in the process; Jonathan did heroic work checking and regularizing my quotations.

Finally, I am grateful to Margaret Bartley for asking me to write this book, and for continuing to trust me to write it as one draft gave way to another. I was recommended to Margaret by the late, great Russ McDonald, who encouraged my work as a 'close reader' from a very early point in my career; I am sorry that he is not here to read this book and I hope that he would have liked it.

NOTE TO THE READER

All quotations are taken from the Arden Third Series editions of Shakespeare except in the case of *All's Well That Ends Well* and *Measure for Measure*, where quotations are from the Arden Second Series editions. In the few cases where I have quoted from Quarto texts or from the Folio edition, I have used the transcriptions given by Internet Shakespeare Editions (http://internetshakespeare.uvic.ca/). Numerals are used to locate particular lines within an act and scene: for example, '*Coriolanus* 5.3.183' refers to Act 5, Scene 3, line 183. All references to the *Oxford English Dictionary* (*OED*) are taken from the online edition (www.oed.com).

PART ONE

CHAPTER ONE

The Title

Overview

The complexity of Shakespeare's dramatic language begins with the titles of his plays, which describe but cannot fully contain the expository and thematic material of their plays. This chapter considers different kinds of complexity in Shakespearean play titles. In section A, I discuss plays where a single word in the title has multiple connotations and is relevant to the play in multiple ways. In section B, I discuss plays where the title implies a focus different from what the play seems actually to be about. In section C, I examine the title-pages of a few plays as they appeared in the earliest printed texts in order to show how titles create expectations about form or genre that change over time.

A.

The word 'errors' in *The Comedy of Errors* refers to the confusions that occur in the city of Ephesus when two sets of long-separated identical twins are mistaken for each other: an error is a mistake. But the verb 'to err' also means 'to wander', and so the 'errors' of the title also refer to the international travel that drives the plot: Egeon's work as a merchant travelling between Syracuse and Epidamnum (1.1.36–43); the voyage from Epidamnum during which Egeon's family was separated by a storm (1.1.62–94); Antipholus of

Syracuse's quest in search of his twin brother, and Egeon's quest in search of Antipholus of Syracuse (1.1.124–39); and Antipholus of Ephesus's arrival in Ephesus by way of Corinth (5.1.355–68). The word 'error' or 'errors' occurs only three times in the play, and in the first two (2.2.190, 3.2.35) it simply means 'mistake': in both cases the context is Antipholus of Syracuse being mistaken for his brother. The third time it occurs, right at the end of the play, it has more of a double sense:

> This purse of ducats I received from you,
> And Dromio my man did bring them me.
> – I see we still did meet each other's man,
> And I was ta'en for him, and he for me,
> And thereupon these errors are arose.
>
> (5.1.384–8)

Antipholus of Syracuse refers not only to his being mistaken by Adriana for her husband, or Antipholus of Ephesus's arrest at Angelo's suit, but also to the wanderings around Ephesus that arose from mistakes – as when, for example, Antipholus of Ephesus sent Dromio of Syracuse to Adriana for bail money (4.1.102–14). 'Errors', then, describes the action of *The Comedy of Errors* in at least two different but closely related, and congruent, ways. In so doing, it is similar to the word 'well' in *All's Well That Ends Well*, which can refer both to the reconciliation and promises of future happiness with which the play's complicated action is resolved (all ends, and will be, 'well') and to the magical healing of the king's disease (Helena makes the king 'well') that causes most of the complications.

Sometimes a word in a Shakespearean title will describe the play's action in two different, closely related, but not exactly congruent ways. A good example is the word 'shrew' in *The Taming of the Shrew*. The 'shrew' of the title is, most obviously, Katherine: Petruccio makes this explicit at 4.1.199, as does Hortensio at 5.2.194. According to the *Oxford English Dictionary* (*OED*), the word was a conventional, misogynistic label for a 'woman given to scolding or railing', especially 'a scolding or turbulent wife' (*OED* 3a). At the same time, 'shrew' was also, and originally, a term used to describe a 'wicked, evil-disposed, or malignant man; a mischievous or vexatious person' (*OED* 1a). The play begins with the introduction of a character, Christopher Sly, for whom this label might certainly be appropriate, and it is equally possible that Petruccio's behaviour, especially after he and Katherine are married, might seem as 'shrewd' (*OED* 1a) as his wife's. Sly is at least temporarily 'tamed' by the prank played upon him by the rich lord who finds him outside the tavern, and Lucentio's incredulity about Katherine's transformation at the end of the play (5.2.195 – his own wife, Bianca, has just proved unexpectedly shrewish) at least leaves open the possibility that Petruccio himself has been 'tamed' by his wife's performance of obedience. Is 'shrew' a fair label for Katherine? Does she act any more 'shrewdly' than Petruccio, or, for that matter, her sister Bianca? Can either Katherine or Petruccio really be 'tamed', and is a 'tame' wife what Petruccio most desires in any case? Is Katherine's transformation any more real or less temporary than Sly's? These are questions the play keeps before us at virtually every turn of its action, and our answers to them depend in large part upon our interpretation of the relation between the play's precise yet vague title, where 'the shrew' is left unnamed, and the diverse situations dramatized that it might describe. Similar examples might be found in *The Two Gentlemen of Verona*, where the word 'gentlemen' is sometimes a merely descriptive term for Valentine and Proteus and at other times a term we might use to critique their behaviour; or in *A Midsummer Night's Dream*, where the word 'dream' might refer to any one of several related actions in the play (Bottom's affair with Titania, for example, which he thinks of as a dream; or the lovers' confusions, which they remember only dimly after being put to sleep by Oberon), or to the entire play itself (see Puck's epilogue, 5.1.409–22).

B.

What do the titles *The Comedy of Errors, All's Well That Ends Well, A Midsummer Night's Dream, The Taming of the Shrew* and *The Two Gentlemen of Verona* have in common? None of them contains a personal name. Here as elsewhere in Shakespeare – and perhaps especially in those plays that take their names from proverbial or colloquial phrases (*Love's Labour's Lost, Much Ado About Nothing, Twelfth Night, or What You Will, As You Like It, Measure for Measure* and *All's Well*) – a certain vagueness or openness is the ground of multiple possible meanings. Most of Shakespeare's plays, including his histories and tragedies (but only three of his comedies), have titles that contain personal names. In most of these titles, the names are merely descriptive, announcing to the reader or spectator the main focus, and often the genre, of the play: *Pericles, Prince of Tyre*, for example, or *The Most Lamentable Tragedy of Titus Andronicus*, or *The Life and Death of King John*. In some cases, the name in the title stands in a more oblique relation to the action of the play: Cymbeline, Henry IV and Julius Caesar are all important to the plays that bear their names, but what these plays are most concerned with is, respectively, the love of Innogen and Posthumus, the wild youth of the future Henry V and the tragic history of Marcus Brutus. The double focus, or parallel structure, achieved by plays in which the title character is not the main character is a productive site for analysis.

King Cymbeline, in the opening scene of the play that bears his name, precipitates the action of the love plot when he banishes Posthumus for marrying Innogen; and in the final scene he presides over the revelations and reunions that make that marriage acceptable. The play is 'his' insofar as it is about his family. But between the first scene and the last, Cymbeline is present in only four scenes, and these are primarily concerned with the political relationship between Britain and Rome. In 2.3, he prepares to receive the Roman ambassador. In 3.1, he meets this ambassador, Lucius, and, encouraged by the queen and Cloten, refuses any longer to pay the tribute that Britain, as a Roman colony, owes to Rome. This puts the two countries on a course for war, and that crisis coincides with the king's belated discovery (in 3.5) that his daughter has fled the court. Cymbeline's woes increase when his wife falls ill and Cloten leaves the court to pursue Innogen: he appears, in 4.3, completely overwhelmed by events. The political and military action to which King Cymbeline is essential is certainly not irrelevant to the love plot; the war between Britain and Rome is, after all, the cause of Posthumus's return to Britain. But neither is King Cymbeline's casting off the yoke of Rome so integral to the play (we do not understand it as a plot point until 3.1) that it is impossible to imagine Innogen and Posthumus triumphing over misunderstanding without it; and indeed, in writing this play Shakespeare took the two stories – that of Cymbeline's reign and that of a lover made jealous by a wager – from different sources. To ask the question 'Why is this play titled *Cymbeline*?' is to seek out the logic of Shakespeare's dramatic construction, to answer the invitation to interpretation presented by parallel but disparate plots.

Through subtle juxtaposition, Shakespeare implicitly treats Britain's political troubles and Innogen's sexual troubles as analogies for one another. The scene (3.1) where the queen boasts to Lucius that Britain's natural defences and courageous inhabitants twice thwarted Julius Caesar's attempted invasion (14–33) follows immediately upon the scene where Posthumus fantasizes that Iachimo, when seducing Innogen, 'found no opposition / But what he looked for should oppose, and she / Should from encounter guard' (2.5.17–19) – that is, he felt only the resistance of Innogen's hymen as she gave herself willingly to him. So too the scene in which Posthumus is goaded by Iachimo into gambling on Innogen's chastity (1.4) is the scene in which we first hear, rather obliquely, about the Roman diplomatic mission to collect tribute; here, Posthumus also boasts of the courage of the Britons in the face of Julius Caesar's invasion. Of course, Innogen does not yield to Iachimo, while Britain did fall to Caesar. Between these three scenes the play intertwines sexual and international politics metaphorically and suggests, by analogy, that resistance is always a greater virtue than yielding. Sexual and international politics become more literally intertwined in the later part of the play when Posthumus returns to Britain, and the question whether resistance is the greater virtue returns with surprising complexity in the final scene, when Innogen's forgiveness of her father and her formerly jealous husband occurs alongside Cymbeline's decision to 'submit to Caesar, / And to the Roman empire' (5.5.459–60).

The foregoing paragraphs do not explain 'why' *Cymbeline* is called *Cymbeline*; rather, they model an analytical method that allows you to see the Britain–Rome plot and the Innogen–Iachimo plot not only as separate plots, and not only as parallel plots, but also as two versions of the same theme. The most likely reason that Shakespeare titled the play as he did is that he drew some of the material from the same source – Raphael Holinshed's *Chronicles of England, Scotland, and Ireland* (1577) – from which he drew material for his other English history plays, and it was conventional to name plays about English history after the monarch during whose reign the play's action takes place. That is also why the two parts of *Henry IV* are titled as they are; *Julius Caesar* provides a Roman variation on the convention – and it is also possible that a play so titled would have seemed more likely to draw spectators to the theatre than one called *Marcus Brutus*. However conventional these play titles are, Shakespeare exploits the convention (as he does in all his dramatic and poetic writing) to maximum effect: when the action diverges from what the title implies, a reader or spectator is given multiple perspectives from which to interpret the action.

C.

The titles of Shakespeare's plays are not always what they seem to be. A little research can reveal surprising new layers of implication in them. The play that your modern edition calls *King Henry VI, Part 2* was given the title *The second Part of Henry the Sixt, with the death of the Good Duke Humfrey* in the 1623 edition of that text. Humphrey, Duke of Gloucester was Henry VI's uncle; his spectacular murder in the third act is represented as part of a grand betrayal of the king by his former favourite, the Duke of Suffolk. The play's title, then, gestures towards a particular historical narrative, where the death of the 'Good Duke' is central to an understanding of Henry VI's reign. The 1623 title is shorter than, and significantly different from, the title given to the play's earliest text, which was printed in 1594:

> *The First part of the Contention betwixt the two famous Houses of York and Lancaster, with the death of the good Duke Humphrey: And the banishment and death of the Duke of Suffolk, and the Tragical end of the proud Cardinal of Winchester, with the notable Rebellion of Jack Cade: and the Duke of York's first claim unto the Crown.*

In this title, King Henry VI is absent altogether – crowded out by the tumultuous events that troubled the middle of his reign. The title suggests that a king does not only make but can also be subsumed by history; the frenetic action of the play bears this suggestion out.

Like *King Henry VI, Part 2*, the earliest text of the play we know as *King Lear* (printed in 1608) also has a very long title:

> *M. William Shakespeare His True Chronicle History of the life and death of King Lear and his three Daughters. With the unfortunate life of Edgar, son and heir to the Earl of Gloucester, and his sullen and assumed humour of Tom of Bedlam*

Lear was a legendary king, but his life and reign were (like Cymbeline's) recorded in Holinshed's *Chronicles*. The early title-page of *Lear* insists upon the play's historical veracity ('*True Chronicle History of the life and death*'), and it also advertises the play's connection to another dramatization of the history, first printed in 1605 but first performed at least a decade earlier than that. This play was called *King Leir*, and its title-page read as follows:

> *The True Chronicle History of King Leir, and his Three Daughters, Gonorill, Ragan, and Cordella*

Perhaps the most important thing to know about *King Leir* is that it has, following Holinshed, a happy ending: Cordella does not die, and Leir is restored to the throne. The 1608 title-page of Shakespeare's *Lear* gives little hint of the radical change Shakespeare made to a well-known story; indeed, it might actually be concealing the change in order not to spoil the terrible, tragic surprise. Only in the 1623 edition of *Lear* do we find the title with which we are familiar:

> *The Tragedy of King Lear*

The difference between the earlier titles and the later one might represent the loss of an essential double focus for the later audiences for whom *Lear* was now a popular, familiar play: by 1623, and forever after, it was no longer possible to hope that Lear and his most beloved daughter might be reconciled, and his kingdom restored; you knew the play was a tragedy from the moment you started to read it.

Conclusion

As the first word or group of words that you encounter when reading a Shakespeare play, the title is always worth reading closely, even when it might seem straightforward. The 'nothing' in the ostensibly throwaway title *Much Ado About Nothing* is a pun on both 'noting' (that is, watching and overhearing – activities that drive much of the play's plot) and 'vagina' ('no-thing', that is, 'no penis'). *The Tragedy of Othello, the Moor of Venice* rather conspicuously omits the name of the play's other (and arguably more) tragic figure, Desdemona. And the original titles *The Tragical History of Hamlet, Prince of Denmark* (1603 and 1604) and *The Tragedy of Hamlet, Prince of Denmark* (1623) imply a political focus that is somewhat different from the familial focus that most modern readers bring to the play, and that is expressed in the commonly shortened title, *Hamlet*, which is the name of both the prince and his father. Thinking about how a play's title both does and does not describe its expository and thematic material allows you to enter into the play both with a sense of what to expect, and a readiness to redefine your expectations, of the action as it unfolds.

CHAPTER TWO

Stage Directions

Overview

As much as they are complex works of poetry, Shakespeare's plays are also scripts for theatrical performance. Any good close reading of the language of the plays must be informed by an awareness of how that language might sound as it is spoken by actors, and what actors might do as they speak it. Reading a Shakespeare play while imagining it being performed is not an easy thing to do. To do it well you need at least three things: (1) some basic knowledge about the theatres and theatrical conventions of Shakespeare's time, (2) some general idea of how Shakespeare's plays are performed in the contemporary theatre and (3) the ability to imagine the different ways in which any speech might be delivered or any scene might be staged. For the purposes of this book, I assume that you will get the first two of these things from the Shakespeare course you are taking, from the other books you are reading and from your own visits to the theatre. The third thing is what I will model in this chapter. Like the meanings and potential meanings of what they say, the meanings and potential meanings of what Shakespeare's characters do are often equivocal, contradictory and complexly layered. I will offer some ways of describing and analysing these complex layers by showing you how to read stage directions.

It is important to note at the outset that virtually all of Shakespeare's stage directions must be understood as provisional. Printed play-texts from Shakespeare's time are notoriously unsystematic in their marking of entrances and exits, in their naming of the characters who come onto or go off the stage and in their indications of what characters are supposed to do. Modern editors must constantly supply directions and names, and even actions and gestures, in order to help readers visualize the action. A vivid original stage direction such as '*Holds her by the hand, silent*' (*Coriolanus* 5.3.183) seems extremely significant precisely because it is so rare; but even then we cannot be sure whether it is something Shakespeare himself wrote, or whether it was a notation added to the play-text during rehearsal and preserved in print, or whether it was added by the editors of the 1623 text of *Coriolanus*, because they remembered the gesture vividly from the play's first performances almost fifteen years earlier. Whatever its origins, this stage direction records both something the character does and an idea about the play – about the character performing the gesture, about his relationship to the characters around him and about the significance of gesture itself. All stage directions, even mundane ones, and even those added by modern editors, work similarly to record ideas about character and performance. They are, therefore, an easy and productive place to begin reading closely the language of Shakespeare's plays in action.

Working simultaneously with original stage directions, modern editorial additions and conjectures, and the complex relations between them, I have structured this chapter around the physical movements of characters in and through plays. Section A is about entrances; section B is about where characters go and what they do when they are onstage but not talking; section C is about exits.

A.

Every Shakespeare play begins with the same word, printed in italic font: *Enter*. Characters must come onto the stage in order for the play to begin. The order and manner in which they come onto the stage is significant. At least two kinds of close reading, textual and theatrical, are necessary to describe, define and analyse the action and the relationships between the characters signalled by an entrance. I will start with textual close reading.

Here is how the first entrance, and the first lines, of *The Taming of the Shrew* appear in the text of that play printed in 1623:

> *Enter Begger and Hostes, Christophero Sly.*
> *Begger.*
> ILe pheeze you infaith.
> *Host.* A paire of stockes you rogue.
> *Beg.* Y'are a baggage, the *Slies* are no
> Rogues.

The initial stage direction makes it look as if the hostess's name is Christophero Sly, which is obviously not the case; Sly is the name of the beggar. Perhaps the printer made an error, and the name *Christophero Sly* was meant to be printed on the second line, together with *Begger*, in order to give the character a name before he spoke the play's first line. Some modern editions print the line this way:

Enter Beggar [Christophero Sly] and Hostess

This preserves the original direction as much as possible while making a useful clarification. One reason the original direction might be important to preserve, or at least to know about, is that it seems to give some indication of how Shakespeare thought about the character: primarily as a *Beggar*, and then (and only parenthetically) as a man with a name. In his second line, Sly makes much of his name, and part of the scene's comedy lies in the contrast between his obviously beggarly identity and his claims to aristocratic ancestry. We might, then, argue that, like the similarly unnamed hostess, the beggar is primarily a character-type, and that this inaugural stage direction strikes an important keynote for the entire play, preparing us to think of the characters not as 'real people', but *as* theatrical characters, exaggerated for precise effects. (That hypothesis would gain some support from the fact that the main action of the play is presented as a play staged by a troupe of actors visiting an aristocratic household.) In this light, we might say that the stage direction as it appears in the most recent Arden edition –

Enter Christopher Sly and Hostess

– slightly shifts the emphasis towards the realistic, as do virtually all modern editions when they change the beggar's speech-prefix from

Beg. to *Sly*. Instead of taking the 1623 stage direction's external view of the character, these emendations ask us to inhabit Sly's point of view, to take his word for who he is.

You can, then, read original stage directions (usually provided in the textual notes if they are altered in the modern text), modernized stage directions and the interplay between them for indications they give of possible interpretations of the play. Such reading can and should extend beyond the opening scene, of course. The stage directions in the 1623 text of *Shrew*, for example, most frequently call the play's main female character *Katerina* (the name her father uses) when they direct her to enter; a little less frequently call her *Katherine* (the name she says she prefers); and only very occasionally call her *Kate* (the name Petruccio uses). The speech-prefixes of the 1623 text, however, always designate her as *Kate*. Most modern editions opt for more consistency than this, but different modern editions are differently consistent: the Pelican edition, for example, uses *Kate* for both stage directions and speech-prefixes while the Arden uses *Katherina*. Especially when read against the inconsistency of the 1623 text, these editorial choices subtly but obviously invite a reader to adopt a particular view of who the character is. And it is possible to see even the inconsistency of the 1623 text as offering a similar invitation: *Kate* is used to direct the character to enter in all of the 'taming' scenes – that is, the scenes at Petruccio's house after the wedding; the character is then called *Katerina* again when she enters for the final time and speaks at length about the duties of a loyal wife. My point here is not to argue that stage directions, whether original or modern, encode definite interpretations of the characters they refer to: we don't even know if Shakespeare himself wrote the stage directions we have for his plays, and the stage directions in any given modern edition are frequently the result of a negotiation between the editor's desires, the publisher's house-style and the editorial history of the text. My point is, rather, that stage directions are as complexly legible as anything else in a play-text: reading any instance of '*Enter* ... ' closely can illuminate, complicate or contradict your interpretation of characters and their actions.

My increasingly tight focus, thus far, on the words – and in particular the *names* – printed on the page is in danger of obscuring an important fact about plays: when you see a play, you do not see the stage directions, and you often do not know who a character is until he or she, or someone else, tells you who he or she is. When Shakespeare wrote *The Taming of the Shrew*, he had in mind an audience for whom the experience would be new, occasionally puzzling and frequently surprising: novelty, puzzlement and surprise are fundamental elements of a pleasurable theatrical experience. It is worthwhile, as you read a Shakespeare play, to try to imagine yourself in the position of someone seeing it performed for the first time – as well as in the position of a playwright calculating effects for people who don't know exactly what to expect. A good place to undertake this kind of imaginative experiment is the first moments of a play's first scene, where it is easiest to see the work that the play has to do in order to make itself happen.

The stage direction calls them *Beggar* (and/or *Sly*) and *Hostess*, and their clothing might tell us something about their identities, but for the first five lines of the play, the only thing we know for certain about them is that they are a man and a woman quarrelling. Are they married? Is the woman the *shrew* of the title? Is the man? Are we witnessing a moment of *taming* in progress? I think all these impressions and questions are meant to flash through a spectator's mind in the first few seconds of the play. At line 6, when the hostess asks Sly if he plans to pay for the glasses he broke, we might realize that theirs is more of a business relationship than a personal one, but a detailed explanation of the dispute is not given until lines 83–7 of the second Induction. The play's first dozen lines give us few clues about the kind of action that is to follow. What they do give us is a glimpse of the male–female conflict that the play's title might promise as the subject of the play; moreover, they introduce questions of dominance (does the beggar or the hostess win this round of the fight?), of origin and status (would Sly be a different person if he really were descended from the 'Conqueror'?) and of the relation between economic, social and personal relationships (are these people fighting over love? money? status?) that will recur throughout the play. In the simplest terms, from the moment the characters enter, and both before and after we know who they are, the play asks us to think about the beggar and the hostess in terms that are closely related to those in which we will think about Petruccio and Kate.

B.

After the hostess leaves, Sly is made the object of an elaborate prank: he is told by a bored and mischievous lord that he is himself a lord and has been confined to his chamber for fifteen years while suffering under the delusion that he was a beggar. Dressed in fine clothes, waited upon by servants and presented with a wife (actually a boy-servant dressed as a woman), Sly then takes his place as a spectator of a play being performed at the lord's house by some travelling actors: this play is the story of Katherine and Petruccio. It is unclear what happens to Sly after this point. He is given a couple of lines at the end of 1.1 (prompted by a servant, who notes that the beggar seems to be falling asleep), but then lapses into silence, and is not given any lines even after the play he is watching ends. If you are reading the play, it is easy to forget that Sly is present and even, perhaps, that he was ever present in the first place.

Modern theatrical productions of *Shrew* often make Sly quite visible in, or even incorporate him into, the action of the play: sometimes he cheers or boos at various moments in the play, or comically falls in love with his disguised-boy wife as he is captivated by the onstage romance; sometimes he disappears from his seat above or alongside the stage only to reappear on the stage as Petruccio; or he falls asleep for the duration of the play, and then returns to centre-stage after it is all over, waking in front of the tavern where he began (shaken awake by a policeman, perhaps), and realizing that 'the taming of the shrew' has all been his dream. Such interpolations have no warrant in Shakespeare's text, but they are nevertheless the result of a useful and productive form of close reading: the director or the actors have read the play with a strong awareness of Sly's absent presence. They have kept in mind his final stage direction – *They sit and mark* (1.1.252) – and have read the play wondering what his reactions and his actions might or should be, wondering whether there is any way of explaining – over and above the parallels between Sly, Petruccio and Katherine – why he was brought onto the stage in the first place.

An important part of reading stage directions closely, then, is learning to remember who is onstage when, and learning to imagine what effect silent but visible characters might have on the action and your interpretation of it. Here is a great stage direction from near the beginning of the long opening scene of *Titus Andronicus*. I quote from the most recent Arden edition, which closely follows the 1594 text of the play.

> *Sound drums and trumpets, and enter two of* TITUS' Sons, *and then two men bearing a coffin covered with black, then two other* Sons, *then* TITUS ANDRONICUS, *and then* [, *as prisoners,*] TAMORA, *the Queen of the Goths, and her* [*three*] *sons,* [ALARBUS,] CHIRON *and* DEMETRIUS, *with* AARON *the Moor, and others as many as can be. Then set down the coffin and* TITUS *speaks.* (1.1.72)

The capitalized names (indicating characters who speak) and the few words inserted in square brackets are modern editorial conventions meant to clarify for a reader some relationships among the characters that will only gradually become clear to a spectator. As with the opening stage direction of *Shrew*, it is worth attempting, before we go any farther into the action, to preserve or recapture some sense of the uncertainty that almost always attends a theatrical entrance. Is it possible, for example, on this crowded stage ('*as many as can be*'), to tell Goths from Romans, Titus's sons from Tamora's, prisoners from victors? Quite possibly the Goths are dressed differently from the Romans, and are chained or guarded with weapons; but it is equally possible (not least because bringing characters on in chains is a theatrically complicated thing to do) that these high-ranking and noble captives are brought on ceremonially, almost as peers. They are, after all, guests at the funeral of Titus's sons. And very quickly in the play, indeed in this very scene, the Goths will be given (and take full advantage of) their freedom in Rome; moreover, Tamora will marry the emperor, turning Titus's victory upside down. One of the play's main thematic concerns is the difficulty of distinguishing civilized Romans from barbarous Goths. Through the modern edition's clarifications we can see that vital thematic confusions are embodied in the movement of characters onto the stage.

The action that follows from this stage direction deliberately and elaborately exacerbates the problem of being certain about political and familial relationships. Titus and his sons sacrifice one of Tamora's sons, and she objects vehemently, which is clear enough. But then Titus proclaims Saturninus emperor and tries to give him his daughter Lavinia's hand in marriage against her will. Lavinia's lover Bassianus, disappointed that he was not chosen emperor, insists on his right to Lavinia and is backed by Titus's sons, one of whom Titus himself kills. Both Rome and Titus's family are now divided against themselves. Then the emperor Saturninus, furious at Titus's sons, forgets about Titus's support of his right (both to the throne and to Lavinia) and takes the Queen of the Goths as his wife. Tamora now plays the completely unexpected role of peacemaker between the emperor and his general; at the same time, more predictably, in a speech whispered to her husband, she promises to 'massacre' the entire Andronicus family (1.1.455). All of this happens in a single, long scene. Groups of characters come and go (Titus's sons take Alarbus offstage to sacrifice him and re-enter after having done it; Saturninus and Tamora exit to 'consummate our spousal rites' and re-enter afterwards), but nearly all of the characters who were onstage at the beginning of the scene are onstage at the end; the stage is just as crowded, that is, but the alliances and conflicts between the characters are now completely clear – and are almost exactly the opposite of what we might expect them to be.

Every character introduced in the stage direction quoted above speaks at least once in the scene's first 500 lines, with one exception: 'AARON *the Moor*'. With dark skin and, very likely, an extravagant or exotic costume, this character probably stands out in the crowded entrance at the beginning of the scene. He is clearly neither Roman nor Goth; if he is bound or chained, his identity as one of the war-captives will be clear, but if he is not, we might as easily assume that he is affiliated with either army. A modern reader or spectator is likely to assume that Aaron is a slave or a servant, even if he is lavishly attired; an early modern spectator would probably have been more likely to assume that Aaron was a mercenary (as Othello is for the Venetians), or perhaps even an African or Middle Eastern king, allied with one army against the other. The political allegiance, at least, of this exciting, mysterious figure will become clear (if it is not already) at line 303, when a stage direction calls for him to enter along with Saturninus, Tamora and her sons – all of whom had briefly left the stage during the scuffle over Lavinia. He accompanies these characters offstage for the imperial wedding and returns with them at line 403. Perhaps, through all these movements, his silence creates the impression that he is in fact a servant or a mercenary – and perhaps even a supernumerary, that is, a character whose purpose is merely to create some sense of historical or geographical verisimilitude. Perhaps a spectator never expects Aaron to speak, only to serve as a protector of the Goth queen's person through the first scene and then to disappear once the Goths are securely established in Rome. Alternatively, perhaps the actor playing Aaron conveys through his silence a sense of watchfulness and potential energy; perhaps he suggests that he will be more integrally involved in the action than he currently is, but that he is waiting for just the right moment. We must wait with him.

Whatever we think the actor playing Aaron might manage to convey in the opening scene, it is one of Shakespeare's great theatrical devices to keep him silent for over 500 lines, and then to give him the stage to himself, and a soliloquy that is, more than anything else, a love poem.

> ... Aaron, arm thy heart and fit thy thoughts
> To mount aloft with thy imperial mistress,
> And mount her pitch whom thou in triumph long
> Hast prisoner held, fettered in amorous chains,
> And faster bound to Aaron's charming eyes
> Than is Prometheus tied to Caucasus.
> Away with slavish weeds and servile thoughts!
> I will be bright and shine in pearl and gold,
> To wait upon this new made empress.
> To wait, said I? To wanton with this queen,
> This goddess, this Semiramis, this nymph,
> This siren that will charm Rome's Saturnine
> And see his shipwrack and the commonweal's.
>
> (1.1.511–23)

Everything we might have thought in the first scene about Aaron as a servant, slave, prisoner or king is here brought to the surface in a confused, erotic form: Tamora has been a prisoner of *his* charms; no longer a captive of the Romans, he is free to 'wait upon' her, but what he serves is her sexual desires; she will charm and captivate Saturninus, destroying the 'commonweal' of Rome and, presumably, taking it for herself to rule with Aaron. In this love-fantasy, Aaron is a king after all.

After his soliloquy, Aaron is as loquacious and focused for the remainder of the play as he was silent and ambiguous in the opening scene. To readers as much as to spectators he is *the* character to watch and listen to in the final scene, in which he is treated by the Romans as the 'breeder' of all the 'dire events' that have taken place (5.3.177). Conferring extraordinary theatrical power on a figure who is silent in, marginal to or even absent from the action was one of Shakespeare's favourite things to do. We see another version of it in *Titus* with Tamora, who disappears from 2.3 until 4.4, but is revealed, in 4.2, to have given birth to Aaron's child. 'The empress,' says the nurse who brings the news to Aaron, 'bids thee christen it with thy dagger's point' (71–2). This chilling order from the new mother almost takes your breath away. If we've forgotten about Tamora amidst the frenetic action of the previous two acts, we won't make that mistake again: she is literally back with a vengeance in 4.4, and replaces Aaron as Titus's main antagonist until the end of the play.

Two closely related variations on the silent Aaron and the absent Tamora are Polonius in *Hamlet* 3.4 and Julius Caesar in *Julius Caesar* 3.1 – each of whom dies early in the scene and must remain lying on the stage for approximately 200 lines while the other characters move and speak around him. It is surprisingly easy for a reader simply to forget about the physical presence of Caesar or Polonius once the character has been killed off in a stage direction. To actors as well as characters, however, the bodies are real and must be dealt with; even the most silent characters must be read as integral to understanding the complex social relationships represented in the play. 'Lend me your hand,' Antony says at the end of the scene to a servant who must help him '[bear] this corpse / Into the market-place' (*Julius Caesar* 3.1.291–7). 'I'll lug the guts into the neighbour room,' Hamlet says at the end of his scene (3.4.210) – and adds, with grim comedy, 'Goodnight, mother' (215). She probably won't lend a hand.

C.

Aaron the Moor leaves Rome in Act 4 to protect his child – both from the Romans and from its mother. Unluckily, he is then captured by a soldier who is part of a Goth army now led by Lucius, the exiled son of Titus Andronicus. Aaron has left Rome only to be brought back again; this process of exit and re-entrance is repeated when Lucius brings the Moor before the emperor in the final scene. At the beginning of 5.3, having returned to Rome with his prisoner, Lucius immediately gives an order to his uncle Marcus:

> ... take you in this barbarous Moor,
> This ravenous tiger, this accursed devil;
> Let him receive no sustenance, fetter him
> Till he be brought unto the empress' face
> For testimony of her foul proceedings.
> And see the ambush of our friends be strong:
> I fear the emperor means no good to us.
>
> (5.3.4–10)

Lucius plans to surprise the emperor's banquet and confront Tamora with her captive lover, who has confessed to conspiring with the queen in the destruction of the Andronicus family. In order to prepare his soldiers ('the ambush of our friends') and make the surprise as effective as possible, Lucius must send Aaron offstage almost as soon as he has brought him on. Aaron hisses a curse at Lucius, but Lucius does not take the bait; rather, he simply reiterates his order, now to his soldiers: 'Sirs, help our uncle to convey him in' (15). Following what must be, to Lucius, the completely unexpected violence of the next 150 lines, Marcus must rather anticlimactically order 'that misbelieving Moor' to be brought back in and 'adjudged some direful slaughtering death, / As punishment for his most wicked life' (142–4). Aaron is brought on for perhaps as few as twenty lines, allowed one final villainous speech and then hauled off to be buried 'breast-deep in earth' (178) as the play ends and everyone leaves the stage. Once the dominant force on the stage, precipitating or managing its most violent actions and drawing to himself the spectator's terrified admiration, Aaron now has barely enough time to say the kinds of things we expect him to say before being led off the stage again. The rapidity with which his forced exits follow upon his forced entrances shows that the Romans have to a large extent succeeded in reducing Aaron to a kind of prop, a mere symbol for all the play's violence. He has become the exact opposite of the ambiguous figure he was when he entered in the play's first scene.

Aaron's exit and re-entrance in *Titus* 5.3 are not marked in the original texts of the play, but they are precisely indicated by the dialogue: Lucius orders his men to 'convey him in' at line 15, and we learn from Marcus at 123 that the 'villain is alive in Titus' house'. At 143 Marcus orders some men to 'hither hale that misbelieving Moor', and at 176–7 an anonymous Roman speaks, clearly having just brought Aaron onto the stage: 'You sad Andronici, have done with woes. / Give sentence on this execrable wretch.' Meanwhile, Lucius, Marcus or some other Roman holds Aaron's child (see line 119), who will have been brought onstage by Lucius at the beginning of the scene. Shakespeare very carefully keeps Aaron offstage, separate from his child, during the climactic slaughter; perhaps the sight of this slaughter, and the thought of his child being raised in its aftermath, is a shock even to Aaron, and perhaps this explains why he has relatively little to say, and nothing at all to say about his child, before the play ends. Whether he is chastened or gleeful at the sight of all the bodies onstage, whether strangely indifferent to or silently but visibly frightened for his child, he is now a reflection of, or a yardstick for, our own reactions.

Another version of this reflective function can be seen in Shylock, whose final exit in *The Merchant of Venice* is marked but does not occur exactly where we might expect it to. At the end of 4.1, when the defeated Shylock asks permission to leave the court and promises that he will, when it is sent to him, sign the deed bequeathing his estate to Jessica and Lorenzo, the duke replies coldly, 'Get thee gone, but do it' (4.1.393). Here we might expect a direction for Shylock to exit. But in both of the play's early texts (1600 and 1623), that direction is delayed for three more lines. Shylock apparently lingers onstage long enough to suffer further abuse from the relentless Gratiano, who taunts him about his imminent forced conversion to Christianity.

> In christening shalt thou have two godfathers.
> Had I been judge, thou shouldst have had ten more,
> To bring thee to the gallows, not to the font.
>
> (4.1.394–6)

If the words of Gratiano throughout the play are grating and mean-spirited, they are particularly so at this moment, where they fantasize an even crueler judicial punishment – Shylock's hanging – after the sham trial has already run its course. Shylock exits in silence; whether or not there is a pause to allow this silence to be felt before the duke speaks his next, incredibly casual line – 'Sir, I entreat you home with me to dinner' (397) – the timing of the exit seems either to create or to confirm the feeling that the scene's action has passed well beyond the bounds of justice.

The lack of a marked exit makes it possible to speculate that something similar to what happens in *Merchant* might happen as well around Malvolio's famous exit line in *Twelfth Night*: 'I'll be revenged on the whole pack of you!' (5.1.371). Malvolio speaks this line after all the people he hates have told him how they methodically set out to humiliate him. According to every modern edition I have seen, including the most recent Arden, Malvolio exits immediately after speaking this line. No exit direction is provided by the 1623 text. The modern conjecture of an exit is based on a line that Duke Orsino speaks shortly after Malvolio: 'Pursue him, and entreat him to a peace' (373). Presumably Malvolio would not need to be pursued if he were still onstage. While it would be hard to imagine a staging of this scene in which Malvolio does not exit, there is at least one alternative moment for him to leave. This is after Olivia's line, which immediately follows his promise of revenge: 'He hath been most notoriously abused' (372).

In the most usual staging of the scene, Malvolio storms off as he speaks, or as soon as he has finished speaking, his line; then there is a heavy silence onstage (because everyone feels guilty), or a smattering of uncomfortable laughter (because everyone hopes Malvolio is not serious), or sometimes peals of unconcerned laughter (because no one takes Malvolio seriously), and then Olivia speaks her line – sounding chastened, or worried, or as though she's still enjoying the joke. In either case (or in any combination of them), Malvolio assumes that no one will take him seriously; any confirmation or contradiction of that assumption – by Olivia laughing as loudly as the rest, for example, or Olivia making others realize that the joke has gone too far – keeps Malvolio where he has been throughout the entire play: out of the loop. To delay Malvolio's exit by just one line might have a subtle but powerful theatrical effect. Imagine (for example) that, after his exit-line, he hesitates just long enough to convey that he is hoping someone will stop him from leaving; everyone is laughing and no one pays attention to him, for they assume that he has gone, and they are enjoying the mean-spirited energy of the Clown's dismissal of him; but Malvolio catches Olivia's eye, and when his reproach causes her to stop laughing, the others stop laughing as well; now Olivia speaks her line, which is a somewhat abashed (or even a haughty and businesslike) acknowledgement, to the steward himself, that he will remain her steward – that she, and everyone in the play, must continue to live with him. Exit Malvolio.

Conclusion

Shakespeare's most famous stage direction is probably the one that occurs in the middle of *The Winter's Tale*: '*Exit, pursued by a bear*' (3.3.57). Having carried out Leontes' order to leave his infant daughter exposed to the elements, Antigonus flees before the onslaught of a savage beast. Offstage, he is eaten. An entire industry of scholarly inquiry has arisen around the stage direction: did Shakespeare's company use a real bear? If the bear was in fact a man in a bear-suit, was it a realistic or a stylized costume? Is this a comic moment or a terrifying one? What experience did early modern Londoners have of bears? And so forth. These five words, wildly unexpected, seem to hold a world within them. One reason the stage direction is so compelling is that, like the one from *Coriolanus* with which this chapter began, it is unusually specific. One reason that it feels so full of possibility is that it is simultaneously a direction for an entrance (the bear's), an onstage action (Antigonus's flight, the bear's pursuit) and an exit (bear and man). To work out what it does for the play, why it is in the play at all, you have to decide upon so many things: personnel, costume, tone, movement, timing. Your treatment of any one of these things affects all the others.

'*Exit, pursued by a bear*' makes clear what is involved in reading any stage direction closely – including paying as much attention to what is *not* happening onstage as to what is. For, as you puzzle out the surprising, frenetic, possibly even comic activity of the bear-chase that moves the play from one geographical location and generic mode to another, it is easy to forget about the other figure who enters with Antigonus but does not exit with him. While a fierce creature devours Antigonus out of view, a helpless creature lies fully in view, uncertainly awaiting rescue. This is the baby, a small, immobile prop that remains onstage, silent and still – possibly for mere moments, possibly for what is or feels like a very long time before the shepherds enter – a focus for all of a spectator's hopes, fears and desires about the play's past and its future. The baby and the bear belong to different worlds within the play, but they are also in a sense the same; we might even say that, as the play begins to turn from domestic tragedy to pastoral comedy, the bear turns into the baby. Each is an ingenious, implausible theatrical device open to a range of conflicting interpretations. The bear might equally be seen as just punishment for Antigonus's following Leontes' terrible order or as a further embodiment of the consequences of Leontes' uncontrollable aggression. To a reader or spectator the baby is an innocent who has been cast out to die, but the Old Shepherd sees the baby much as Leontes does: as a likely product of an adulterous liaison, left for someone else to raise (see 3.3.58–76). Later in the play Antigonus's wife Paulina will hint hopefully that her husband might miraculously return to her (see 5.1.38–44) – an entirely implausible suggestion that is nevertheless hard to dismiss, considering that the baby Perdita, now a young woman who has been raised by shepherds, has been wooed by a disguised prince who is the son of Polixenes, the man Leontes once suspected of cuckolding him with Hermione.

In the dynamic movement between bear and baby, we can see that the energy of Shakespearean stagecraft, like the energy of Shakespearean poetry, resides in the constant oscillation between closely related but different possibilities. As entrance follows exit and scene follows scene, one thing is always on the verge of turning into, or turning out to have been, another.

CHAPTER THREE

Scenes

Overview

Shakespeare's basic unit of dramatic construction is the scene. As the *Oxford English Dictionary* (*OED*) will tell you, the word *scene* in a theatrical context initially referred to *the place of* the action: in the ancient Greek or Roman theatre the *skene* was a structure on the stage that served as a backdrop to the action. In the ancient theatre, action was continuous, so the *skene* was always the same place; that is, the events represented in a play could only take place in a single location, and could only take the same amount of time as the performance itself. In later usage, the word *scene* came to refer to both *a place and a specific time in* the action: a 'subdivision or section of a play ... *esp*. one forming a unit of action taking place at a single location and point in time' (*OED*). In Shakespeare's plays, action is not continuous, so the scene is always changing; that is, the events represented in a play can happen in various different locations and can take place over a much longer time-span than the performance event itself. The scene, for Shakespeare, is one place and one time, but it is also part of a larger whole.

Scenes are clearly marked and numbered in modern editions of Shakespeare plays, as are the larger units, acts, that comprise groups of scenes. As will be discussed in more detail in Part Two of this book, act and scene markers are useful to the close reader because they help you see the architecture of the play: the first act establishes the setting and the main dramatic problem, while the second act generally introduces a secondary problem; the third act brings the two problems together and the fourth is concerned with the consequences of the collision; the fifth act unwinds the threads and produces a resolution. Act and scene markers are also somewhat anachronistic. If we were ever to discover the manuscript of a Shakespearean play, it would probably not contain marked act or scene divisions: no Shakespeare play printed during the playwright's lifetime contains marked act *or* scene divisions, and only about half of the plays published in the 1623 Folio contain *both* act *and* scene divisions (in most, the acts are marked but not the scenes). Rather than acts and scenes, Shakespeare the dramatic architect seems to have thought primarily in terms of entrances and exits. What your modern edition marks as a scene begins when one or more characters enter and ends when the stage is clear. Plays in Shakespeare's time most commonly relied upon dialogue rather than movable scenery to establish the location of any given scene and its temporal relation to those that precede it. Thus, while the place and time of Shakespeare's dramatic action are always changing, they are also continuous: as each new scene begins, we must wait to hear how it is different from or similar to the scene that has come before it. Watching Shakespeare's plays unfold in a series of entrances and exits, in a dynamic movement between different groups of characters separated by brief moments where the stage is empty, is a constant process of interpreting the relation between the part and the whole.

You can read a scene, or series of scenes, just as closely as you can read a single line, a speech or a series of images. That is what this chapter is about. In section A, I describe and analyse the way some individual scenes are constructed. In sections B and C, I offer some ways of describing and analysing the relation between one scene and another, and between individual scenes and the entire play. These two sections are different from one another in that section B demonstrates how you might analyse an apparently irrelevant scene in relation to those around it, while section C demonstrates how you might analyse obvious continuities between sequences of scenes.

A.

Shakespeare's scenes do not follow any set pattern, but in his scene construction, as in his poetic language, the playwright has certain habits and predilections: he particularly likes to build scenes around repetition and variation – around things that happen more than once. Consider, for example, the final scene of *Othello*, nearly 400 harrowing lines in which Desdemona is repeatedly pronounced dead (85, 90), only to revive briefly and die again (118–26); Othello is twice disarmed (237–8, 284), only to reveal that he has a third weapon concealed (354–8); Othello learns that Cassio has been wounded but not killed (112–18) and, later, stabs but does not kill Iago (285); Montano enters with Iago twice (163, 280); and Othello twice falls on the bed where he killed Desdemona (195, 357).

Shakespeare also likes to manipulate the dynamic relation between movement and stillness, a full stage and an empty stage. The final scene of *Othello* begins with a terrifyingly intimate conversation between Othello and Desdemona in their bedroom. Starting with Emilia's shouting (84), the quiet scene is gradually filled with noise and people – Emilia, Iago, Montano, Gratiano and an unspecified number of anonymous officers. Emilia is killed by Iago, who flees, with Montano and the rest in pursuit, briefly leaving Othello alone once again with a woman's corpse. Just as Emilia had shouted earlier to Othello while he was locked in the room with the dead Desdemona, now Gratiano shouts to Othello while he is locked in the room with the dead Emilia (253–7). The room then fills up again: Montano and Iago return, accompanied by their officers as well as Lodovico and – of all people! – Cassio. Everyone arrives just in time to witness the spectacle of Othello's suicide.

Othello 5.2 is one of several very long scenes in a play that seems to have been written to test both the actors' and the spectators' endurance. Shakespeare is, however, equally capable of constructing even a very short scene out of complexly related, dynamically arranged entrances and exits. The first scene of *The Tempest*, not quite 70 lines long, begins with just two characters onstage, the Master and the Boatswain. The Master almost immediately exits. The solitary Boatswain is then surrounded by people: first the Mariners who enter at line 4 and are there to try to keep the ship afloat in the storm, and then '*Alonso, Sebastian, Antonio, Ferdinand, Gonzalo, and others*' – the passengers who come on deck from their cabins to tell the Mariners how to do their job. The Boatswain switches his attention between these two groups, ordering the Mariners to assist him – 'Yare! Yare! Take in the topsail' (6), 'Cheerly, good hearts' (26) and rebuking the passengers because they 'do assist the storm' (14) with their meddling. Confident in his abilities, indifferent to titled authority, concerned above all with self-preservation but willing to linger with Gonzalo for a chat about the limits of human authority in the face of nature's fury, the Boatswain, with his frank way of speaking, insists on the likeness between the two groups of men on the ship whose manners and costumes will insist on their difference. 'You are a councillor,' he says to Gonzalo, 'if you can command these elements to silence ... we will not hand a rope more' (20–3). It is better to be a sailor than a councilor in a sea-storm and, like the sea itself, the Boatswain cares little 'for the name of king' (17); and yet, even with all his competence and confidence, he cannot prevent the ship from splitting. All men are powerless before the storm.

After putting Gonzalo in his place, the Boatswain rushes off to do more work, barking an order to the passengers: 'Out of our way, I say.' Presumably (as the footnote in the Arden edition suggests), the Mariners exit with the Boatswain at this point. It seems safe to presume this – and I will do so because it is useful for the reading of the scene I want to develop – because the Boatswain uses the plural possessive pronoun *our*, and because a stage direction at line 51 directs the Mariners to enter again. It is worth noting, nevertheless, that the stage direction in the 1623 text reads *Exit* (singular) rather than *Exeunt* (plural), which would suggest that only the Boatswain leaves, while the Mariners remain behind; perhaps you can develop your own reading of the scene based on the idea that the Mariners who enter are present throughout (there is no direction in the 1623 text for them to leave) and that those who enter at line 51 are additional mariners.

Whatever you might think, I like to think that the Mariners and Boatswain all leave the stage together at line 27, because this means that Gonzalo and the other noble passengers now have the stage to themselves briefly while, offstage, the '*tempestuous noise of thunder and lightning*' called for in the scene's opening stage direction continues. Literally out of his element, Gonzalo puts himself in the hands of superstition and fate (27–31) before following the Boatswain's orders and – presumably accompanied by the other nobles – returning below-decks to his cabin. At this point the stage will be empty, and it might seem, if only for a second, that the scene is over, and that we will be left to imagine the fate of the ship, or to hear about it at some point later in the play. When the Boatswain re-enters, it is clear that the scene, like the ship's troubles, is not over. This method of essentially squeezing two scenes into one is a means of conveying the intensity of the dramatized experience – the feeling of both endlessness and an all-too-imminent end that one might well get when trapped in a boat that is likely to sink at any moment.

With the re-entrance of the Boatswain we can see clearly Shakespeare's fascination with repetition and variation. It is almost as though the play has started all over again. 'Yare! Lower lower,' the Boatswain calls (33–4), in an echo of line 6, and then Sebastian, Antonio and Gonzalo re-enter. 'Yet again?' the Boatswain says in exasperation (38). Sebastian insults him, and the Boatswain, echoing what he said to Gonzalo at 22–4, replies simply: 'Work you, then' (41). Gonzalo once again comments, as he did in lines 27–32, on the fact that the Boatswain seems to be immune from drowning. The repetition suggests that the noble passengers cannot get their heads around the fact that they have no control over either the elements or the sailors, whose job it is to keep those elements from harming them; for as long as the storm goes on, the nobles will continue to shuttle between their cabins and the deck, trying to find some way to exert their will.

Of course the storm cannot go on forever, and the variation Shakespeare introduces into this repetitive sequence comes itself in the form of a repetition: this is the second entrance of the Mariners, now '*wet*' (50). With this stage direction, the tenor and tone of the dialogue change. Now there is no vigorous argument, only resignation and terror: 'What, must our mouths be cold?' says the stunned Boatswain (51), imagining a death by drowning. 'Farewell, my wife and children! – Farewell brother!' (61) is the cry of mariners and passengers from within the boat (that is, from offstage), and the previously enraged Antonio can now hope only to 'sink with th' king' (63) – who is, as Gonzalo has noted, preparing himself for death with prayers. The stage directions are ambiguous about exits through to the end of this scene. Neither the Mariners nor the Boatswain is given a direction to exit: in a footnote, the editor of the Arden edition suggests that they might 'fall to their knees in prayer on deck'. When I imagine the scene, I see the Boatswain and Mariners exiting probably around line 61, perhaps shouting as they go: 'We split, we split, we split!' The stage, increasingly full of people since line 36, has begun to empty again; now only Antonio, Sebastian and Gonzalo remain. Sebastian is given an exit direction at line 64, and most editors suggest that Antonio should leave with him. I disagree. I think that the scene should end with Gonzalo speaking his wish for 'an acre of barren ground' to Antonio. This line is an echo of the Master's line at the beginning of the scene, where he instructs the Boatswain to avoid running the ship 'aground'. The echo is underscored by the fact that the scene begins and ends symmetrically with two characters onstage.

The first scene of *The Tempest* and the last scene of *Othello* are alike in being divided into several separate sections, each of which might seem to be a scene in itself; in their dynamic movement between noise and silence, many characters and few characters; and in having a symmetrical structure based on repetition and variation. These scenes are exemplary of what Shakespeare tries to do with any scene: he tries to represent at least two separate actions that are both parallel and intertwined (the ship's crew speaks one kind of language, the noble passengers another, and the Boatswain links the two); and he tries to make the end similar to the beginning while also making it clear that a real change has taken place between beginning and end.

Of course, not all of Shakespeare's scenes work exactly this way. *Henry V* 3.1, for example, consists of a single speech. This is Henry V's famous exhortation to his soldiers at the battle of Harfleur: 'Once more unto the breach, dear friends, once more' (3.1.1). There is definitely a symmetry to this scene, in that Henry V's solitary speech – most likely spoken directly to the spectators – is accompanied by the noises of battle ('*Alarum*', according to the stage direction at the beginning of the scene) and the raising of '*scaling ladders*' against the walls of the city. The scene dramatizes the king's words becoming action and extends his dominion to the theatrical audience itself. At the same time, there is something asymmetrical about the scene because only one character speaks. And the content of his speech – a vision of extraordinary national unity – is to some extent given the lie by the action that follows it. Henry probably exits at the end of this scene, though he is not given an exit direction. To the accompaniment of trumpets and guns ('*Alarum and chambers go off*'), the actor charges offstage to represent the king leading the way once more unto the breach. Does a spectator think that the scene is over at this point? Quite possibly not, for immediately following upon Henry's exit is the entrance of three English soldiers, who are also some of the king's old friends: Nym, Bardolph and Pistol. For a moment, we might think that these characters occupy a time and location that are continuous with the king's speech – just as, when the Boatswain enters a second time in *The Tempest* 1.1, we realize that Gonzalo's exit did not signal a shift in time and location after all. The first words of this new scene echo the first words of the previous one: Bardolph shouts 'On, on, on, on, on! to the breach, to the breach!' as though inspired by the king's words. But neither Pistol nor Nym nor the Boy who accompanies them is at all interested in endangering himself in battle, and the Boy explains, at 3.2.28–53, that all of them, even Bardolph, are cowards. These characters are then displaced on the stage by Fluellen, Jamy and Macmorris – representatives of (respectively) the Welsh, Scottish and Irish contingents of Henry's army – who do not seem even to have heard Henry's speech (they are concerned only with the orders of the Duke of Gloucester; see 54–64) and whose disagreements about military strategy hardly correspond to the king's vision of national unity (see especially 119–34). The entrances of 3.2, then, are not continuous in time and location with 3.1. The action of 3.2 takes place not only some time after Henry's speech and on some other part of the battlefield, but in something like a separate moral universe: its characters balance but also seem completely disconnected from the lofty rhetoric of 3.1. That scene is over after all: it was simply a self-contained speech, perhaps even a somewhat empty performance; maybe we were the only ones who really heard it.

Othello 5.2 is a scene that keeps extending itself; *Tempest* 1.1 is a scene that keeps turning in upon itself; *Henry V* 3.1 is a scene whose fullest meaning and implications lie in its relation to other scenes. These three kinds of scenes – one of which is from the end of its play, one from the beginning and one from the centre – provide a good, though certainly not comprehensive, overview of Shakespearean scenes and some approaches you might take to describing and analysing them. The most important example in this section is probably the one from *Henry V*, because the general principle I have used it to demonstrate – that the meaning of one scene depends upon its relation to other scenes – is true and useful for all Shakespeare's plays. It is as true for *The Tempest* – whose tightly wound, somewhat elliptical first scene is followed by a leisurely, highly expository second scene – as it is for *Othello*, whose brutal final scene, set in the bedroom, is preceded by an equally brutal scene that takes place in the streets. Scenes in a Shakespeare play are like words in a Shakespeare speech: each one both anticipates and changes in the light of what comes after. To read any one scene closely, you need to read a whole series of scenes closely. This is what I will discuss in the next section.

B.

Antony and Cleopatra 3.1 is a surprising scene. Its first stage direction (as it appears in the 1623 text) calls for the entrance of one character whom we've barely seen before and another, now dead, whom we've neither seen nor heard of (nor will again) throughout the play. The living character speaks in an elaborately formal, heroic idiom that is used by no one else in the play.

> *Enter* VENTIDIUS *as it were in triumph, [with* SILIUS *and other Romans, Officers and Soldiers,] the dead body of Pacorus borne before him.*
>
> VENTIDIUS
> Now, darting Parthia, art thou struck, and now
> Pleased fortune does of Marcus Crassus' death
> Make me revenger. Bear the King's son's body
> Before our army. Thy Pacorus, Orodes,
> Pays this for Marcus Crassus.
>
> (3.1.1–5)

What is Ventidius talking about? The attentive reader or spectator might recall that Ventidius has appeared twice before, both times in the company of Antony (2.2.14–16, 2.3.39–41), and that both times Antony told him that he would be sent to Parthia; and the historically informed reader might know something about the Roman wars with the Parthian empire, and that Marcus Crassus, a member of Julius Caesar's triumvirate, was killed in battle against the Parthians while Ventidius, a general under Antony, had great success in Parthia. But this is a lot to piece together in a play that is otherwise completely unconcerned with Parthian affairs. Moreover, Shakespeare seems to try to make it as difficult as possible to piece things together. The lines 'Thy Pacorus, Orodes, / Pays this for Marcus Crassus', for example, contain three proper names that occur nowhere else in the play. One is the name of the dead man who is just being brought onstage (there is no reason a spectator should know that the dead man is Pacorus), one is an absent and dramatically irrelevant figure (Orodes, king of the Parthians) and the third is a dead and dramatically irrelevant Roman ruler (Crassus). All of a sudden, in the middle of the play, reader and spectator are asked to comprehend and infer the importance of a great deal of new information very quickly. If Ventidius were to become an important character after this point, or if Antony's wars with Octavius and love of Cleopatra were, for the remainder of the play, shadowed by the Parthian wars, we might readily see, in retrospect, the importance of this scene. But neither Ventidius nor Parthia is mentioned again; the scene stands alone. What is it doing in the play?

Brilliantly, the footnote to the entrance stage direction in the Arden edition notes that 'whereas the previous scene leads up to the carrying out of the drunken Lepidus, this one starts with the carrying in of the dead Pacorus'. The previous scene, 2.7, involves a celebratory feast aboard Pompey's boat, where the triumvirs Antony, Caesar and Lepidus celebrate their newfound (but, as it turns out, short-lived) unity as well as the (also short-lived) truce they have made with Pompey. Almost totally self-contained in terms of the plot, 3.1 nevertheless resonates with the scenes around it. In the party scene, as the Arden editor says in the same footnote, 'the commanders are celebrating their spurious concord', while in 3.1, 'the subordinate [i.e. Ventidius] is loyally carrying out his orders'. We might elaborate these points a bit further: the heroic idiom in which Ventidius speaks at the beginning of 3.1 is in stark contrast to the trivial, drunken exclamations that conclude 2.7:

ENOBARBUS
Hoo, says 'a! There's my cap!
MENAS
Hoo! Noble captain, come!

(2.7.135–6)

Pompey notes that he has reason to avenge his father (who was killed in Egypt after Julius Caesar drove him out of Rome) but passes up the opportunity, while Ventidius sees himself as the avenger of the death of Marcus Crassus. At the same time, honourable as his actions may be, Ventidius's laboriously expressed, elaborately humble desire to serve Antony but not provoke his envy (12–27) seems almost quaint, or perhaps simply bizarre, given what the play shows us about Antony, and in comparison to the clear-sightedness with which two other subordinates, Agrippa and Enobarbus, talk about their generals after the party on Pompey's boat is over (3.2.1–20, 51–8). The footnote in the Arden edition also notes that 3.1 is frequently cut in performance, which may not be defensible in structural terms but is perhaps understandable given how opaque it is compared to everything around it. The scene is in the play in order to show us what is not in the play – heroism, unquestioning loyalty, the honourable exercise of power – and, perhaps, to suggest that if these things were in the play, the play might not be as interesting as it is.

At the end of 3.1 Ventidius says that he will write to Antony, to 'humbly signify what in his name, / That magical word of war, we have effected' (30–1). The play is full of news and letters from this point on: Cleopatra gets a description of Octavia in 3.3; in 3.4 Antony sends Octavia back to Rome, because he has heard that Caesar 'hath waged / New wars 'gainst Pompey' and 'Spoke scantly of me' (3–5); in 3.5 Eros delivers to Enobarbus the 'strange news' (2) that Caesar has imprisoned Lepidus on a trumped-up charge of treason; and in 3.6 Caesar complains of a report that Antony and Cleopatra have had themselves 'publicly enthroned' (5) in Alexandria. All the alliances cobbled together and celebrated in the second act are now falling apart. Amidst the many letters and reports through which the fraying of the empire can be traced, Ventidius's good news disappears: if Antony ever receives his lieutenant's letter, he says nothing about it (though, it should be noted, the historical Antony did reward the historical Ventidius with a triumphal procession for his victories against the Parthians); and no one else in the play delivers or comments upon the news of Pacorus's defeat. Most likely you, the reader, will also forget about the first scene of Act 3 before the play is over; the excitement and romance of this play have nothing to do with military victory.

C.

Shakespeare wrote many scenes like *Antony and Cleopatra* 3.1: scenes that initially seem not to fit, but which, by means of close-reading techniques such as the ones I have employed in the foregoing paragraphs, can be shown to be integrally related to the play as a whole. It is also possible, of course, to use these techniques to understand and analyse the intricately unified structure of obviously important scenes. Consider, to take a famous example, the middle section of *Hamlet*. The scene in which Hamlet is amazed at the Player's ability to seem *to be* something he is *not* (2.2), is followed by the scene in which Hamlet ponders the question *To be or not to be* (3.1) while his uncle and Polonius spy on him to try to determine whether he *is or is not* mad. In the next scene (3.2) Hamlet uses a play – in which the actors pretend *to be* something they are *not* – in order to work out whether his uncle *is or is not* guilty. Immediately after the play, in 3.3, Hamlet comes upon his praying uncle and decides not to kill him because, through the *act* of prayer, Claudius seems *to be* in the process of repentance. But the moment Hamlet leaves, we learn from Claudius that his prayers are not working: 'My words fly up, my thoughts remain below' (3.3.97). He *is not* what, to Hamlet, he *seemed to be*, and to himself he cannot even seem, much less be, what he would like God to think he is. These four scenes are connected by repetitions and variations on the idea of *seeming* and *being*, an idea that is introduced explicitly by Hamlet at the beginning of the play when he tells his mother that, in his sorrow for his father's death, there is no *seems*, only *is* (1.2.76).

You could almost certainly extend the analysis I have begun with these four scenes in *Hamlet* right through the play. *Hamlet* is a very intricately constructed play, and little of it is likely to strike a reader or spectator as not fitting, in the way that *Antony and Cleopatra* 3.1. does. The closest thing to a scene that seems irrelevant is probably the first half of 2.1, where Polonius instructs his servant Reynaldo to spy on Laertes while Laertes is in France: what Laertes gets up to in France is of little concern to anyone, including Polonius, after Reynaldo exits at line 73. Polonius is here trying to do what Claudius and Hamlet will both spend the play trying to do: discover whether someone is what he seems to be. We never find out whether Polonius's suspicions were justified – though Laertes' behaviour when he returns to Denmark suggests that they might not have been – so this thread of the plot stands in ironic relation to the main plot: on the one hand Polonius does not find something he seems sure will be there, and on the other hand Hamlet and Claudius are certain they have discovered something about each other, but neither can be certain what it is. Most of Shakespeare's plays work like *Hamlet*: different scenes represent different but closely related characters talking about or working through an idea that is prevalent throughout the play. The second act of *Julius Caesar* provides another vivid example. The centre of 2.1 is Portia's argument with Brutus about whether or not she should be privy to whatever he is planning; in 2.2 we see Calphurnia and Caesar arguing about Caesar going to the capitol, and Calphurnia claims to have knowledge of the future that Caesar blithely ignores; in 2.3 Artemidorus reads aloud a letter he has written to Caesar which reveals that he knows everything about the conspiracy; and in 2.4 Portia frantically employs Brutus's servant Lucius, and interrogates the Soothsayer, in order to get some information about what is happening at the Capitol. These four scenes – including the rather surprising and unexplained walk-on by the well-informed Artemidorus – are unified by an idea of *knowing* in the same way that the scenes I have discussed in *Hamlet* are unified by an idea of *being*.

In some plays, however, scenic and dramatic unity are created by expressing or implying relationships between characters who occupy separate scenes and know nothing of one another. In *A Midsummer Night's Dream*, for example, each of the first three scenes introduces a group of essentially independent characters: the noble Athenian lovers in 1.1; the Athenian labourers in 1.2; and the fairies in 2.1. The fairies know of both the other groups, but neither of those (with the partial exception of Bottom) ever knows of the fairies; the labourers are preparing a play for the duke, but know nothing of the young lovers, and the young lovers know nothing of them. The brilliance of *Dream* lies in

Shakespeare's ability to keep the first two groups completely separate – putting each at the mercy of the fairies in a different way – until they meet at the dramatic performance that concludes the play. In vital tension with this separation, Shakespeare repeatedly puts the three groups in thematically analogous or related situations. So the first three scenes all dramatize contests of authority: between Egeus, Theseus and Hermia; Bottom and Quince; and Titania and Oberon. And all three are concerned with broken love affairs: between Hermia and Lysander, Helena and Demetrius; Pyramus and Thisbe; and Titania and Oberon. The complex entanglements experienced by each group of characters in the course of the play all involve problems of seeing. More subtly, they also turn on problems of servitude: Egeus's desire to punish Hermia for disobeying him is thwarted by his obligation to obey the duke; Bottom and the Mechanicals are rehearsing a play in order to serve the duke at his wedding (and are treated rudely by the noble guests when they do so), but when Bottom briefly becomes Titania's lover, one of the perks is being waited on by her fairies (see 3.1.170–96 and 4.1.1–38); and Oberon and Titania are quarrelling about who will get to possess a changeling child, whom Titania currently keeps as an 'attendant' (2.1.23) but whom Oberon wants to make a 'knight of his train' (2.1.25) or his 'henchman' (2.1.121). Dramatizing three realms of existence or experience – mortal and noble, mortal and common, and supernatural – while keeping them realistically separate but poetically interconnected, Shakespeare suggests that fickle desire, voluntary servitude and class rivalry are, if not immutable facts, then at least woven together in the fabric of natural and supernatural experience. Like *Antony and Cleopatra*, which represents both the reality of heroism and its impossibility, and like *Hamlet*, whose characters are caught up in the fundamental problem of being, *A Midsummer Night's Dream* manages to achieve something like a universal scope.

Conclusion

A spectator has no advance warning, in *A Midsummer Night's Dream*, that Puck is going to turn Bottom into an ass. The mechanicals are rehearsing a scene from *Pyramus and Thisby* and Bottom, as Pyramus, exits with a promise to re-enter: 'by and by I will to [Thisby] appear' (3.1.82). To this, Puck, of whom only the spectator is aware, says 'A stranger Pyramus than e'er played here!' (83), which gives little hint of what's to come; for all we know, Puck might simply be speaking as a dramatic critic – Bottom, a bad actor, makes a strange Pyramus indeed. When Bottom, having missed his cue, returns to the stage wearing what will obviously be a prop ass-head, there is no reason for a spectator to assume that he has actually been transformed into an ass. We might more readily assume that he has raided the props-box to play a joke on his friends, or that he is costumed for yet another part; surely a play that has a part for a lion and a wall might have a part for an ass. At this moment, two scenes are overlaid upon one another – the scene of the performance of *Pyramus and Thisby* and the scene of the performance of *A Midsummer Night's Dream* – and only gradually are they disentangled, or do we realize that they had been entangled at all. As we realize that Bottom has been transformed into an ass, the 'performance' of *Pyramus* is transformed into the 'reality' of *Dream*.

Shakespeare's scene construction in *Dream* is particularly ingenious and self-conscious, but it is also representative of what he seeks to achieve in all his plays. Divisions between scenes are both just as definite as, and much less definite than, the editorial divisions in your modern edition imply. Consider, finally, the moment linking the first and second acts of *Troilus and Cressida*. At the end of 1.3 Nestor speaks of stoking the quarrel between Agamemnon and Achilles; at the beginning of 2.1, Ajax and Thersites enter quarrelling.

NESTOR
Now, Ulysses, I begin to relish thy advice,
And I will give a taste of it forthwith
To Agamemnon. Go we to him straight.
Two curs shall tame each other; pride alone
Must tar the mastiffs on, as 'twere a bone. *Exeunt*

Enter THERSITES *[followed by]* AJAX.

AJAX
Thersites!

THERSITES
Agamemnon – how if he had boils, full, all over, generally?

AJAX
Thersites!

THERSITES
And those boils did run (say so) did not the general run, then? Were not that a botchy core?

AJAX
Dog!

THERSITES
Then there would come some matter from him. I see none now.

AJAX
Thou bitch-wolf's son, canst thou not hear? Feel then.
Strikes him.

(1.3.388–2.1.11)

The two scenes move between the highest and the lowest degrees of the Greek army, between formal poetry and obscenity-filled prose, but in a sense there is no distance between them. The snarling of dogs can be heard all over the camp. The beginning of any scene is a moment of transformation, not only of the bare stage into a specific time and place, but of the preceding dramatic and poetic material into something different from or larger than itself. The end of any scene is both a transformation of its beginning and an opportunity to imagine how its poetic and thematic material will return in a new form after the stage is cleared.

CHAPTER FOUR

The Whole Play

Overview

The work of close reading is deconstructive: as you have seen in the preceding three chapters, and as you will see over the next eleven, it involves slowing down the reading experience to see what the play looks like as it unfolds one word, one line, one scene, one act at a time. It involves breaking a play down into its component (often very minute) parts and, in many cases, isolating those parts from their larger context to see what each one 'does' in itself and in relation to others. For this deconstructive work to be meaningful, it must always also be reconstructive: even to select and define the minute component parts you want to analyse, you must have some larger (if only general) idea of what the play that they come from is and does. The discoveries you make by focusing on a single word, line, stage direction or scene must be used to express, complicate or even contradict your first impressions of what the play's language and action mean or can mean.

In this chapter, I argue that a critical interpretation of, or simply a critical idea about, a play must be the starting point for close reading, even though it is something that will inevitably change in the course of close reading. You need to have an idea of how the whole play might be read before you start reading it closely. To bear out this argument, I will focus in this chapter on a single play, *1 Henry IV*. I have chosen this play because it presents obvious challenges to the student reader that can be met through critical analysis. In section A, I discuss some of the work that might be done to develop a productive overall impression of the play. In section B, I illustrate a method for achieving, relatively quickly, a detailed grasp of the play's structure and the relation between that structure and some of its component parts. In section C, I demonstrate how an interpretation based on close reading can and must take into account elements of the play that initially seem incongruous or extraneous. The overall goal of the chapter is to trace the process whereby a general impression of a play becomes, by way of close reading, a specific interpretation – and how that interpretation lays the groundwork for further close reading.

A.

The first thing to do when you decide to read a Shakespeare play is to read the whole play. Then read it again. The first time, just read it quickly: the goal is to get an overview of its shape, a general idea of what happens in it and a sense of which parts you will have to return to, either because they are confusing or because they might reward close reading. The second time, read it more slowly – but not too slowly: keep a pencil in your hand to mark words, lines and passages that seem baffling or significant; reread any passages that seem particularly interesting; try to pay attention to words or images or ideas that recur and vary throughout the play; think about the relation between the play's title and its action; try to use the stage directions to imagine various scenes or moments in performance, or in different possible performances; try to pay attention to the arrangement of scenes, and make a note of any scenes that seem out of place or extraneous. It may be useful, between the first and second readings, to read a plot summary of the play, simply to allow you to worry less about what is going on. It is important to remember, however, that plot summaries are always only partial, and that they often make things sound clearer than they actually are in the play. Confusion and uncertainty, as much as excitement and surprise, are an inevitable part of the experience of reading and analysing a Shakespeare play. Allow yourself, in your first encounter with a play, to be comfortable with uncertainty, both about what is taking place and about what are the most important things to focus on and think about; you don't want to lock yourself in to a particular interpretive point of view before you start reading closely.

After you have read the whole play twice, you should try to come up with a general statement that describes your experience of it. Here is mine for *1 Henry IV*: I don't know which character this play is supposed to be about. Now, this is obviously not much of an argument, but it is a good place to start the project of close reading and analysis, because it registers a vivid and truthful impression. I will now make this impression more specific by asking some questions that follow from it and by pursuing some of the implications of their potential answers. Is the play about its title character, Henry IV? He certainly speaks a lot, but he also seems to be pushed to the margins of the action by three other characters who vie with each other, and with other characters, to hold the stage with their words: Prince Hal, Hotspur and Falstaff. Is the play about Prince Hal? At first glance, he seems to be the character to whom the most happens in the play, as he metamorphoses from irresponsible barfly to heroic prince. Yet Prince Hal announces at the end of his first scene (1.2) that he is secretly a heroic prince, and is just waiting to show his true colours; in a way, he simply becomes the thing he has always been and the thing that, as viewers of a history play, we know he must become: the future Henry V. If we are looking for a character to whom much really does happen, we need look no further than Hotspur, who progresses from impetuous rebel to tragic hero by way of loving husband (2.3, 3.1) and political pawn (5.2), and who seems genuinely surprised by the journey. But to say that the play is about Hotspur, Prince Hal's foil, doesn't seem quite right, or at least not without first considering the prince's *other* foil, Falstaff, a character who is not even a historical figure yet whose theatrical, and especially verbal, exuberance are always on the verge of taking over the play. If the play is about Falstaff, then what is it actually *about*?

I have now arrived, through my own uncertainties about the play, at a description of the play's form that is both general and specific: the title character of *1 Henry IV* struggles for prominence with at least three other important characters. Everything these four characters say – and all of them say a lot – demands a great deal of attention and interpretive energy from a reader or spectator, and because the focus shifts constantly between them we must maintain that attention over the course of the play; in the end, it remains uncertain who gets the last word. Once you arrive at this kind of general but specific characterization of the play, I suggest that you hold it in suspension while you turn your attention to the play's language and structure on a more detailed level. This is what I will do now, and I will return to and modify my characterization of the play in order to construct an actual thesis statement about it after I have done some close reading.

B.

If you are uncertain where to start your close reading, the two best places to look are the play's first scene and its last. Parallels and echoes between these two scenes will give you a clear idea of the continuities or patterns Shakespeare is most interested in articulating or tracing in this play. If you look at 1.1 and 5.5 of *1 Henry IV*, you will quickly see that it is a remarkably symmetrical play. Henry IV speaks the play's first lines and also its last; in both his first speech and his last speech, he talks of having just put down a rebellion (it is a rebellion on behalf of Richard II in 1.1, and the Hotspur rebellion in 5.5) and of having more fighting to do. At the beginning of the play, Henry's forces, aided by Hotspur, have recently defeated a Scottish force – and also, aided by Mortimer, defeated the forces of Owen Glendower; at the end of the play, Henry's forces have defeated Hotspur and captured the Scottish Lord Douglas, and they now set out in pursuit of Mortimer and Glendower, who have joined forces. Prince Hal, absent in the first scene, is by his father's side in the final scene, and will accompany the king on the Welsh expedition. Hotspur's uncle, Worcester, also absent in the first scene but referred to by the Earl of Westmoreland as 'malevolent' at line 96, is present in the final scene, and referred to by Henry IV, who sentences him to death, as 'ill-spirited' (5.5.2). Finally, and most elegantly, the issue that preoccupies Henry IV in the first scene is Hotspur's refusal to yield up his Scottish prisoners to the king so that the king may have their ransom money; in the final scene, Prince Hal releases his Scottish prisoner, Douglas, 'ransomless and free' (5.5.28) as a reward for how valiantly he fought.

Structurally, the play ends as it began – the civil war is still not over – but its end is also an inversion of the beginning: Hal has been reconciled with his father and has done something Hotspur could not do. This structure is a large-scale version of the dense, compact passage in which the play introduces one of its main concerns: the relation between fathers and sons. This is what a frustrated Henry IV says in 1.1, when he thinks about how proud Northumberland must be of his son Hotspur.

> O, that it could be proved
> That some night-tripping fairy had exchanged
> In cradle clothes our children where they lay,
> And called mine 'Percy', his 'Plantagenet';
> Then would I have his Harry, and he mine.
>
> (1.1.85–9)

King Henry wishes that he might one day discover that his real son is Hotspur: that would then explain why Prince Hal acts so little like the son of a king. This fantasy of radical transformation is to a large extent enacted over the course of the play as the prince comes, in the final scenes, to embody some of the martial ideals previously associated exclusively with Hotspur. But the passage is also confusing to read and think through, not least because Hotspur and the prince share the same name (and share it with the king himself): Harry. In the king's fantasy, the revelation of one son as the other would be a revelation of *Harry* as *Harry*; the king expresses a wish for his son (Hal) to be more noble by imagining him into the position of a rebel (Hotspur). The passage achieves the inversion it seeks only with difficulty, just as the play struggles in its final moments to reverse all the forces that set its action in motion: not only must the king continue to prosecute his civil war, but Hal is still friends with Falstaff – indeed, has just allowed him to take credit for killing Hotspur.

I have moved, in these two paragraphs, from large-scale structural analysis to a close reading of a single passage. In doing so, I have started to demonstrate that the action of *1 Henry IV* is at the outset, and remains at the end, in a state of suspension: domestic strife is always just on the verge of being (but never actually) quelled; Harry always seems just about to become (but perhaps unable to become) Harry. I believe that this description of the play provides a specific basis for my initial, impressionistic claim that it is hard to decide whom the play is about. Is it more important that Hal is reconciled with his father at the end of the play, or that Falstaff is reconciled with Hal? Is it more important that Hotspur is dead or that the civil war continues? Through close reading on a large and small scale, I have arrived at an argument about the relation between the whole of the play and some of its individual parts. The argument is still a bit general, however, and, in boiling everything down to the relation between fathers and sons, it oversimplifies the play. My goal now is to give a more accurate idea of the play's complexity by expanding the scope of my argument. In order to do this, I will invert what I did at first: I will start with some passage-level close reading and move to an analysis of structure. And my close reading will begin not with a scene (such as the first or the last) that obviously articulates the themes of the entire play, but rather with one that seems, initially, not to fit into the play at all.

C.

The first scene of Act 2 takes place at an inn on the road between London and Canterbury. Here are lodged the travellers whom Hal, Falstaff and their friends will rob in the next scene. None of the travellers appears onstage in 2.1; instead, the scene shows us two carriers – men delivering goods to London who are also staying at this inn – as they prepare their horses and goods in the predawn hours. These characters have nothing to do with the plot of the play; they do, however, briefly encounter the notorious Gadshill (mentioned by Falstaff and Poins in 1.2, where the plan for the robbery was made), who arrives at the inn to confirm with the chamberlain the intelligence he has given the robbers: that some travellers carrying a lot of money will be on the road this morning. In terms of exposition, the scene does nothing for the play other than introduce Gadshill (who will appear in the robbery scene and in the scene at the tavern where Falstaff describes the robbery), and the play would make perfect sense without it. It is a short scene, where the characters speak in familiar, allusive, very detailed terms: 'Robin Ostler' (10), 'chamber lye' (20), 'a gammon of bacon and two races of ginger' (24–5), 'a franklin in the weald of Kent' (53–4), 'eggs and butter' (58). These and other phrases suggest that we are seeing a slice of real life, where the people who pass over the stage have personal concerns that we can only just overhear or catch a glimpse of. It is a different verbal idiom from anything else we get in the play, including the often detailed and opaque language of Falstaff, which, because of its association with the prince, tends to aspire to (and sometimes achieve) a grandeur that feels mythical or allegorical even when it is quite trivial. The first scene of Act 2 is a small scene in a big play. What is it doing here?

To begin to describe the work of a scene like 2.1, I will subject it to the same analytical treatment to which I initially subjected the entire play: that is, I will look closely at its beginning and its end. The scene begins with an expression of haste:

> 1 CARRIER
> Hey-ho! An it be not four by the day, I'll be hanged. Charles's Wain is over the new chimney, and yet our horse not packed. – What, ostler!
>
> (2.1.1–3)

The carrier, telling time by the position of the stars in the sky, is eager to get on the road, and he calls for his horse. The scene also ends with a call to the ostler, framed by Gadshill's witty banter with the chamberlain about the robbery plot they are setting in motion.

> GADSHILL
> Give me thy hand; thou shalt have a share in our purchase, as I am a true man.
> CHAMBERLAIN
> Nay, rather let me have it as you are a false thief.
> GADSHILL
> Go to. Homo is a common name to all men. Bid the ostler bring my gelding out of the stable. Farewell, you muddy knave.
>
> (2.1.90–6)

Gadshill's observation about the 'common name to all men' is an acknowledgement that the chamberlain is right about him being a 'false thief', followed by the philosophical shrug of a rogue: when you get right down to it, he suggests, all men are thieves. The scene is symmetrical and built upon an inversion: it begins with the entrance of an honest, hard-working man and ends with the exit of a cynical thief, each in his turn calling for a horse.

Looking still more closely at the beginning and the end of the scene, and their relation to material around them, you can see that, although

2.1 stands apart from the rest of the play in its setting, characters and idiom, it is also carefully woven into the play's verbal fabric. The last scene of Act 1 concludes, as the first scene of Act 2 begins, with a reference to the time: 'O let the hours be short,' Hotspur says, 'Till fields and blows and groans applaud our sport!' (1.3.296–7). As the Carrier in the next scene is eager to deliver his turkeys to London, so Hotspur is eager to encounter Henry IV on the battlefield. The second scene of Act 2 begins, as the first scene of Act 2 concludes, with a reference to horses and thieves: 'I have removed Falstaff's horse,' Poins reports gleefully to Prince Hal. A few lines later, the exhausted Falstaff, indignant that he has been forced to walk, inveighs against his friend: 'I am accursed to rob in that thief's company' (2.2.10); wittily but unwittingly Falstaff expresses the truth of Gadshill's line about all men being thieves. These connections, which you might see as merely verbal – punning links that allow one scene to turn into another – can in fact be elaborated to express strong thematic lines across the play.

1 Henry IV, especially in the early scenes, and especially on the edges of those scenes, is explicitly preoccupied with time. In the second line of the play, Henry IV tries to find 'a time for frighted peace to pant' the news of his impending crusade. 'What time of day is it lad?' Falstaff asks Hal at the beginning of 1.2, and at the end of this scene Hal presents his plan for gradually revealing his true royal nature as a plan for 'Redeeming time'. The third scene of Act 2 begins with Hotspur reading a letter whose author is reluctant to serve in the fight against Henry IV because 'the purpose you undertake is dangerous, the friends you have named uncertain, the time itself unsorted ...' (9–11); in the second half of the scene, Hotspur, undaunted by the prospect of fighting with a reduced force, is still in a hurry to get to the battlefield. Refusing to tell his wife why he's in such a hurry, Hotspur puts off her playful accusations that he does not love her with these lines:

> Come, wilt thou see me ride?
> And when I am a-horseback, I will swear
> I love thee infinitely.
>
> (2.3.96–8)

Like the carriers, like Gadshill, like Falstaff at the beginning of 2.2, like the prince at 2.2.100, Hotspur's primary goal in his movement onto and off the stage is to get on a horse.

Time and horses: these are the words that give definition to the structure of *1 Henry IV*'s opening movement. They are simple, necessary and expressive words for a history play, where time is the subject of representation and the horse is a never-seen but ubiquitous symbol of status and martial ability. And while Shakespeare finds other subtle and minute ways to connect one scene to another after 2.3 (see, for example, the movement from Falstaff's itemized list of expenses at the end of 2.4 to the divided-up map of England brought onstage at the beginning of 3.1), he returns to time and horses, and recombines them with great thematic resonance, towards the end of the play. In 4.1, Hotspur gets the news that the king has set forth for battle, and he wonders ironically whether he will be joined by 'his son, / The nimble-footed madcap Prince of Wales' (93–4). Somewhat to Hotspur's surprise, Sir Richard Vernon tells him that Hal has, to all appearances, become a real warrior-prince: Vernon saw him

> Rise from the ground like feathered Mercury,
> And vaulted with such ease into his seat
> As if an angel dropped down from the clouds
> To turn and wind a fiery Pegasus
> And witch the world with noble horsemanship.
>
> (4.1.105–9)

Hotspur can hardly bring himself to believe Vernon's vision, but also accepts and relishes the possibility that he might at least have a worthy adversary on the battlefield. 'Come, let me taste my horse' (118), he cries in an enthusiastic echo of his own language in 2.3 and that of other characters in 2.1 and 2.2. He is then challenged to maintain his enthusiasm when Vernon gives him more unexpected news of Glendower:

> I learned in Worcester, as I rode along,
> He cannot draw his power this fourteen days.
>
> (4.1.124–5)

Time, like history, is not on Hotspur's side. Perhaps to his credit, he knows there is nothing he can do to stop its motion: 'Come, let us take a muster speedily', he says, keeping up the urgency that has distinguished him from Hal and Falstaff throughout the play: 'Doomsday is near. Die all, die merrily' (132–3).

The argument that my close reading has led me to is not only that 2.1 is fully integrated into the poetic fabric of the play, but also that its essential elements – horses and time – are expressive of the play's genre and are used by Shakespeare to frame a climactic moment in which two of the play's Harrys begin to change places, and to change their relation to the third. The point of this argument is not to insist that 2.1 is the most important scene in the play, only that it is just as important as any other. What makes the scene distinctive, and seem initially not to fit, is its concern with anonymous characters of a low social class. The inn is very down-market: the carriers are plagued by fleas, and, because they are not provided with a chamber-pot in their room, they have to piss in the fireplace (14–22); Gadshill is a regular and suspicious presence at the inn, and the carriers know him well enough not to lend him their lantern – for fear he might walk away with it – or to tell him their travelling schedule (31–45); the chamberlain accepts kickbacks from thieves for providing information that allows them to accomplish their robberies (90–3). On one hand, you are meant to see this place and the people who frequent it as qualitatively different from the court and the battlefield, the politicians, noblemen and honourable soldiers with which the play is more usually concerned; Shakespeare's dramatic-historical representation of Henry IV's England is all the more accurate because it does not flinch from representing the seamy side of life. On the other hand, you are also meant to see the characters and setting as representative of a historical truth that the political and military action obfuscates: whether it is Henry IV stealing the throne from Richard II and breaking his promises to those who helped him do it; Falstaff, Poins and Gadshill being robbed by their disguised friends as they are in the process of sharing the spoils of the first robbery; Mortimer, Glendower and Hotspur squabbling over how they will share out the kingdom once they take it back from Henry IV; or Prince Hal 'robbing' Hotspur of his youth (5.4.76), England is full of thieves, honest men are always in danger of being taken advantage of, and most horses are overworked and malnourished.

Conclusion

As promised, I have moved from the most minute close reading of 2.1 – focusing on the words and phrases at its very edges – to a series of larger, more general interpretive gestures. It remains only to insist that 2.1 is experienced by a reader or spectator very much as a discrete unit within the play (that is, it does not present itself as a key to interpretation), but also to point out that its discreteness is characteristic of the play's form overall. The class-specific, colloquial language spoken by the characters in this scene may not be spoken by anyone else in the play, but the play as a whole is consistently interested in characters who speak in a very particular, even a peculiar manner: Hotspur, Falstaff and Owen Glendower are the most obvious examples; Lady Mortimer, who only speaks Welsh, and Francis the Drawer, who barely speaks more than one word, are the most extreme and symbolic examples; and Prince Hal is not only able to speak in a number of particular idioms (from tavern roarer to dutiful son to heroic prince) but has deliberately made a study of doing so (see 2.4.4–32). If the play is 'about' any one thing, it is perhaps about language itself as a force that can simultaneously define and divide a nation. My initial general impression – 'I don't know which character this play is supposed to be about' – which I have already revised into something slightly more specific – 'The title character of *1 Henry IV* struggles for prominence with at least three other obviously important characters' – can now be refined into something like a real argument that describes and can enable close reading on a large and small scale: 'The movement of history in *1 Henry IV* is represented disjointedly and in many different voices and idioms; whether princely nobility or cowardly thievery will define the English nation remains a matter of suspense right through to the end of the play.'

PART TWO

CHAPTER FIVE

First Words

Overview

Like the titles and title-pages, the very first words of a Shakespeare play contain a great deal of information about the nature of the action, and that information can almost always be understood in different ways. The first words spoken by any given character are similarly informative and complex. In sections A and B of this chapter, I read closely the first words of two plays and analyse the relation between their opening gestures and all the action that follows from them; the relation is more oblique in the first case and more comprehensive in the second. In section C, I provide a few ways of analysing the first words spoken by characters whose first appearance occurs after the opening scene.

A.

Although a spectator or reader encountering the play for the first time would have no way of knowing it, the characters who appear in the first moments of *The Taming of the Shrew* have no part in the main action of the play; they are only a part of the open-ended 'frame' in which the story of Katherine and Petruccio is presented, and which that story quickly leaves behind. Nevertheless, the first words they speak strike a keynote for the play that will gradually unfold from their entrance.

SLY
I'll feeze you, in faith.
HOSTESS
A pair of stocks, you rogue!
SLY
You're a baggage, the Slys are no rogues. Look in the Chronicles; we came in with Richard Conqueror: therefore *paucas pallabris*, let the world slide. Sessa!
HOSTESS
You will not pay for the glasses you have burst?
(Induction 1.1–7)

An irascible man with pretensions to high status has upset the household of an equally irascible woman, and now the two quarrel in a public street. She says that he should be arrested ('A pair of stocks') and he tells her to shut up ('*paucas pallabris*', i.e. 'few words'). The scene will be replayed, with variations, multiple times by Katherine and Petruccio over the course of the play. The hostess manages, as Katherine does not, to bar her antagonist from her house (he falls drunkenly asleep while she goes to fetch a constable), but Sly, like Petruccio, seems to escape punishment for his antisocial behaviour – at least for now: he is taken into a noble house and treated as a lord (the same word Katherine uses to describe Petruccio in her final speech, 5.2.152). Of course, Sly's elevation is a mere prank, and we must know that he will one day experience, quite literally, a rude awakening; similarly, the incredulity Lucentio expresses about Katherine's taming in the play's final line (5.2.195) suggests that Petruccio's 'victory' might well turn out to be illusory. The first words of *The Taming of the Shrew* set in motion a pattern of gendered conflict and ambiguous resolution that structures the entire play.

Julius Caesar also begins with the entrance of characters who will be peripheral to the main action: two tribunes rebuke a crowd of commoners for their revelry during Caesar's triumphant entry into Rome after his defeat of Pompey. The way in which these characters are peripheral is, however, different from the hostess and Sly in *Shrew*. While the realistic, lower-class English characters of *Shrew*'s opening scene are wholly outside the world of the imaginary, upper-class Italian characters in the taming plot,

Flavius and Marullus and the commoners are fully a part of the Roman world represented in *Julius Caesar*: although the tribunes do not appear again after 1.1, we hear in 1.2 that they have been deprived of their offices (possibly even put to death) by Caesar; and the commoners of the first scene almost certainly reappear as part of the crowds that come onstage in 1.2, 3.1, 3.2 and 3.3. The first words spoken in *Julius Caesar* do sound a thematic keynote for the rest of the play – this is the tension between authority and licence, the state and its people – but they also glance at or anticipate thematic concerns that will become obvious later in the play.

FLAVIUS
Hence! home, you idle creatures, get you home!
Is this a holiday? What, know you not
(Being mechanical) you ought not walk
Upon a labouring day, without the sign
Of your profession?

(1.1.1–5)

Julius Caesar is a play in which characters, like Flavius in this speech, are much preoccupied with the legibility of signs – whether these be prophecy and augury (1.2.24–6, 2.2.38–40, 5.1.77–88), meteorological and supernatural phenomena (1.3.1–129), dreams (2.2.71–107), a man's name (3.3) or the behaviour of soldiers seen at a distance (5.3.28–32). It is also a play in which the importance of particular days is a repeated concern: most obviously the Ides of March (1.2.18–23, 3.1.1–2), but also Cassius's birthday (5.1.71–2) and the 'raw and gusty day' on which Caesar challenged Cassius to a swimming contest (1.2.100–6). In 2.1, Brutus, contemplating the murder of Caesar, asks his servant Lucius to '[l]ook in the calendar' (42) and tell him whether the next day is the Ides of March. His uncertainty is an echo of Flavius's own confusion in the first scene: for, while, the question in Flavius's second line suggests that he thinks the day is *not* a holiday, Marullus reminds him at the end of the scene that it is in fact 'the feast of Lupercal' (1.1.68). *Who are you? What does this mean? What day is it?* These are basic and essential questions asked in the opening moments of, and throughout, *Julius Caesar*.

B.

A play's first words, then, generally contain the raw materials for one or more patterns that Shakespeare will continue to work out in subsequent scenes. In the example of *Shrew*, the first words are part of a pattern of action, and in the example of *Caesar* they are part of an essentially verbal pattern that is used to articulate complex thematic questions in many different situations. The first words of *The Winter's Tale* do some of the same things that we see in *Shrew* and *Caesar* – that is, they sound a keynote and anticipate later verbal and thematic material – and something more as well: they introduce a problem of interpretation that will confront characters and audience alike throughout the play. Again the character who speaks these words is peripheral (he appears only in this scene), but he speaks them to a character (Camillo, a Sicilian lord) who is integral to the plot.

> ARCHIDAMUS
> If you shall chance, Camillo, to visit Bohemia on the like occasion, whereon my services are now on foot, you shall see, as I have said, great difference betwixt our Bohemia and your Sicilia.
>
> (1.1.1–4)

The keynote sounded here is the concern with the relation between, and travel between, Sicilia and Bohemia; and the lines ironically anticipate the unexpectedly terrible action of the next scene, where a 'difference' (in the sense 'dispute or quarrel', *Oxford English Dictionary* 3) between Leontes and Polixenes causes Camillo to make a trip to Bohemia sooner than he expected. The problem of interpretation introduced also has to do with the word 'difference': Archidamus insists that Sicilia and Bohemia are very different places (Bohemia, he goes on to say, will not be able to provide Leontes with nearly as warm a welcome as Polixenes had in Sicilia), but Camillo dismisses this as mere flattery and insists that each place has given and can give as much as the other deserves (24–31). The question debated in the first words of the play is whether Leontes and Polixenes, and their respective countries, are more similar than different, more equals than rivals. It is a question that both the audience and the kings themselves must confront repeatedly and in various forms throughout the play: does Bohemia provide a refuge from or simply a repetition of the problems in Sicilia? Are Leontes and Polixenes starkly different or unsettlingly alike as fathers and as men who love Hermione? Does the final scene, where Polixenes' son becomes the heir to Leontes' kingdom, represent a restoration of their friendship or the beginning of a new phase in their rivalry?

There is something almost riddling about Archidamus's speech: neither here nor in his lines later in the scene can you be exactly sure whether he means that Sicilia is better than Bohemia, or that Bohemia will strive to be better than Sicilia. Archidamus refers to a conversation – 'as I have said' – that has preceded his and Camillo's entrance, so from the play's first words, a reader or listener is in the position of trying to establish, based on imperfect information, the relation between two disparate things. Another riddle, which *Winter's Tale* shares with *Shrew* and *Caesar*, is simply why the play begins this way at all – that is, with a conversation between characters who will disappear, or reappear only infrequently in the remainder of the action. Giving the first words of a play to 'minor' characters is a favourite device of Shakespeare's. The effect is to provide a larger perspective on the main action by, again, asking you to think about the relation between disparate things: what does the revelry of commoners have to do with the world-shaping political violence of *Julius Caesar*? What does a fight between a tavern hostess and a drunken tinker have to do with the courtship of Katherine and Petruccio? Other plays whose first words you might look at in order to consider such questions include *Romeo and Juliet* (a crowd of serving-men exchange bawdy insults); *Antony and Cleopatra* (Antony's friend Philo talks about how Cleopatra has changed the general); and even *A Midsummer Night's Dream* (Theseus and Hippolyta, towards whose wedding the entire plot moves, appear only in the play's first and last scenes).

Of course Shakespeare does not give the first words to peripheral characters in all his plays. *Macbeth* and *The Merchant of Venice*, for example, both open with something like a riddle, spoken by characters who play a major role in the action. So does my final example in this section, *All's Well That Ends Well*. Like the first words of *Macbeth* and *Merchant*, the first words of *All's Well* are interesting not simply because they sound a keynote or anticipate later verbal and thematic material but because they seem to encapsulate the entire play.

COUNTESS
In delivering my son from me, I bury a second husband.
(1.1.1–2)

The widowed Countess of Rossillion is sad that her son Bertram must go to Paris to become a ward of the king; when he goes, she will be as bereft as when her husband died. This is, at any rate, what we gradually come to understand the countess has said as the scene moves forward. By itself, the countess's line is compact and cryptic: the word 'delivering' means 'sending forth', but it can also, in other contexts, mean 'giving birth to', and the countess is evoking that sense to achieve a rhetorical contrast with 'bury' in the second half of the sentence. The joy of sending her son out into the world brings with it the pain of sorrow for a lost loved one. The confusing thing about the second half of the sentence is that the countess imagines Bertram's metaphorical 'death' (that is, her loss of him) by thinking of him as a replacement ('second') for her dead husband. The idea is that Bertram has, since his father's death, been what we might call 'the man of the house', but the vague hint of incestuous desire suggests that the line is saying something more than it reveals.

How do the first words of *All's Well* encapsulate the entire play? Helena has come to love Bertram while living in his house, after her father's death, as the ward of the countess (1.1.35–7); when she confesses this love to the countess (1.3), she must not only acknowledge the class difference between them but also strenuously resist the countess's affectionate insistence that she, Helena, is like the countess's own daughter – Helena does not want to seem to be in love with her own brother. After Helena marries but is abandoned by Bertram, she pursues him into Italy, and her plan to win him again turns on an act of substitution: Helena takes Diana's place in her assignation with Bertram. The resolution of the plot depends upon Helena's 'resurrection' (Bertram has heard that she died) and also her pregnancy. All these elements of the plot – the suggestion of incestuous desire, the substitution of one body for another and the proximity of death and birth (and rebirth) – are compressed into the countess's line, where Bertram has taken his father's place and where his going forth into the world gives his mother both the joyful pain of childbirth (again) and the sorrowful pain of mourning (again).

C.

Shakespeare rarely gives the first words of a play to the title character, and often delays that character's entrance until later in the scene, or a later scene altogether. Notable exceptions to this general rule include *Richard III, Richard II* and *1 Henry IV*. Antonio, the merchant of Venice, speaks the first words of his play, but we do not have any way of knowing, as he speaks them, that he is the title character; and Shylock, arguably a more important character than Antonio, is not introduced until the third scene. Some plays, of course, are not named after characters: we cannot expect anyone in particular to appear at the beginning of *Twelfth Night* or *Much Ado About Nothing*. In *Much Ado*, the lovers who will become the focus of the action, Beatrice and Benedick, are introduced gradually over the course of the first scene, but it is probably not until the second act that we begin to realize that their story will compete for our attention with the unfolding story of Hero and Claudio. The first speech of *Twelfth Night* is spoken by Orsino and seems, in the course of that scene, to inaugurate a plot that will bring Orsino together with Olivia. The character who will actually marry Orsino, Viola, is given the first line of 1.2.

Delaying the entrance of the title character (or the main character) has an obvious theatrical and architectural value. Macbeth's name is spoken in the sixth line of his play, and it is perfectly reasonable to think that either the king who speaks the first line of the second scene, or the 'bloody man' (1.2.1) who approaches him, is Macbeth. Like the witches, however, the king and the bleeding captain are onstage only to talk about Macbeth. When the captain leaves, another character approaches: 'Who comes here?' asks the king (45). Again, I think the spectator or reader is led to expect the entrance of Macbeth, and again that expectation is thwarted. This new character is only the 'worthy Thane of Ross', who is ordered at the end of the scene to confer the title of Cawdor upon Macbeth. It is only in the middle of the third scene, after a cryptic conversation between the three witches, that Macbeth finally enters. His first words are worth the wait: 'So foul and fair a day I have not seen' (1.3.38). Small talk about the weather links Macbeth directly to the witches' riddling incantation, 'Fair is foul and foul is fair', at the end of 1.1. We will probably expect, from the first scene, that the play will trace a close relationship between them. Macbeth's first words begin to give us some sense of just how close this relationship will be, and also how much our understanding of what Macbeth says and does is filtered through the witches. When we hear him speak for the first time, it is as though we have already been party to his thoughts.

The words that so forcefully connect Macbeth to the witches are spoken after he has been characterized (by the report of the bleeding captain) as the most active and loyal of soldiers, and after the witches have made it clear (in the first half of 1.3) that they are involved with other mortals as well – and not exclusively with such weighty matters as kingship and dynastic succession. Is Macbeth already a pawn of the witches, even as he routs the Norwegian army on behalf of the Scottish king? Do the witches have an interest in the political affairs of Scotland, or is the murder of a king no more or less important to them than a squabble over chestnuts? These questions, which have a direct bearing upon the play's representation of ambition, free will and fate, are prompted in large part by the careful positioning of Macbeth's first words.

In *Measure for Measure*, Isabella's entrance is delayed until the fourth scene, and when she enters she confronts the same problem of balancing licence with restraint confronted by the abdicating duke in 1.1, Claudio and Juliet in 1.2 and the duke-as-friar in 1.3 (see 1.3.1–6, where the duke must reassure Friar Thomas that he is not disguising himself in order to pursue a secret love).

ISABELLA
And have you nuns no farther privileges?
FRANCISCA
Are not these large enough?
ISABELLA
Yes, truly; I speak not as desiring more,
But rather wishing a more strict restraint ...

(1.4.1–4)

Like so many Shakespearean scenes, this one begins *in medias res*: we get to hear only a small part of a conversation that has been taking place offstage. If we try to imagine what the characters were talking about before they entered, we might come up with at least two possibilities. On one hand, Francisca might have been trying to persuade Isabella to join the cloistered life by telling her about the many privileges nuns have within the convent. Isabella's reply – that is, her first words in the play – might in this case be interpreted as an expression of disapproval: she wants her life as a nun to be as ascetic as possible, and she hopes that Francisca has 'no farther privileges' to enumerate. Such an interpretation would be consistent with a view of Isabella as morally uncompromising and would allow us to take her next three lines at face value. On the other hand, Francisca might have been describing to Isabella the stark realities, and few privileges, of the cloistered life. Isabella's first line in this case might be interpreted as an expression of surprise – there are 'no farther' privileges than this? – and her next three lines as a back-tracking attempt to insist upon her readiness to become a nun. Such an interpretation would be consistent with a view of Isabella's moral rigidity as a deliberate and difficult repression of a more worldly attitude. We can grant that Shakespeare probably heard the conversation a certain way in his head as he wrote it – that is, he probably knew the meaning he wanted to convey – and also grant that the form in which he chose to convey this meaning is a deliberately equivocal one.

Measure for Measure is a play about the fine line between uncompromising and compromised morality; it is about the difficulty of deciding whether licence or restraint is more desirable or, indeed, whether they are more similar than different. These are issues that any reader or spectator of, or actor in, the play must confront at virtually every turn. Isabella, introduced into the action on the very boundary between the convent and the city, seems particularly to embody these issues, in no small part because of how her first words entangle her in conflicts from which she would expect to remain aloof.

Conclusion

In drama, first impressions are important; a character's first words do much to establish the terms in which we think about him or her and the actions of which he or she is a part. Shakespeare likes his characters to make different first impressions simultaneously. 'Thanks' is the first word Caius Martius (later given the surname Coriolanus) speaks in a tragedy that repeatedly turns on the performance of gratitude and the perception of ingratitude. This word is spoken to his old friend Menenius, who has just hailed him as 'noble Martius'. Martius then turns to the citizens of Rome with a decidedly different tone: 'What's the matter, you dissentious rogues, / That, rubbing the poor itch of your opinion, / Make yourselves scabs?' (1.1.163–5). Othello's first lines are more understated: 'Tis better as it is' he says to Iago as they enter in mid-conversation in the play's second scene, Iago railing against some slur someone made against the general (1.2.1–6). Othello's quiet reply might suggest that he is calmly aloof or hopelessly passive, and in any case will find a stark contrast in the play's final scene, where he smothers Desdemona, wounds Iago and kills himself. By the same token, Othello's fearlessness of Brabantio's objections to his marriage – 'Let him do his spite; / My services which I have done the signiory / Shall out-tongue his complaints' (1.2.17–19) – will find an echo in the lines he speaks before his suicide: 'I have done the state some service, and they know't' (5.2.337). In these examples you can see that first words – both of a play and of its most important characters – not only sound a keynote, setting the tone for all that follows, but also act as a keystone: they hold in vital tension the opposing forces that give the play its soaring shape.

CHAPTER SIX

The First Act

Overview

The purpose of the first act of a Shakespeare play is to introduce all or most of the play's central conflicts and the main strands of action in which they will be dramatized. This purpose can be achieved in a variety of ways. In some plays, the first act introduces two or more strands of action in parallel, and begins to suggest some ways in which the strands are analogous or will be intertwined. In other plays, the first act introduces a single strand of action, usually arising from the relationship between two or three of the main characters, and presents different perspectives on it. Each of these two kinds of first act will be discussed in turn in sections A and B of this chapter. In section C, I discuss some ways in which the first act creates, and both fulfils and defies, expectations about the kind of action that will follow.

A.

The first act of *The Merchant of Venice* gives a systematic overview of the actions and themes that will follow in subsequent acts. Each of the three scenes of *Merchant*'s first act introduces a separate relationship that will be the focus of one of the play's three main strands of action: Antonio and Bassanio in 1.1; Portia, Nerissa and Portia's dead father (with a very brief gesture towards Bassanio) in 1.2; Antonio, Bassanio and Shylock in 1.3. We might distil this further and say that each scene of the first act introduces a different character who occupies a distinct space: Antonio (Christian Venice), Portia (Belmont) and Shylock (Jewish Venice), each of whom speaks the first words of his or her scene; at the same time, the act as a whole entangles them around the figure of Bassanio. All these distinct spaces and the relationships they contain take shape around some form of obligation: Bassanio is not only Antonio's friend but also his longtime debtor (1.1.140–52); Portia is beholden to the terms of her dead father's will (1.2.20–33); Nerissa is not only Portia's friend but also her waiting-woman, responsible for mediating between her mistress and the suitors who flock to Belmont from all nations (1.2.95–100); and Antonio becomes Shylock's debtor on behalf of Bassanio. When Shylock defends the terms on which he has agreed to lend Antonio money – the potential forfeiture of a pound of Antonio's flesh – he suggests that behind this apparently poor business decision lies a desire to be better friends with him:

> A pound of man's flesh, taken from a man
> Is not so estimable, profitable neither,
> As flesh of muttons, beeves or goats. I say
> To buy his favour, I extend this friendship;
> If he will take it, so; if not, adieu,
> And for my love I pray you wrong me not.
>
> (1.3.161–6)

Shylock is almost certainly being disingenuous, but his speech encapsulates the central concern of all three scenes and, indeed, the entire play: this is the complex and often conflicted relation between affection (among friends, kin, or masters and servants), obligation or indebtedness, and material gain.

The schematic structure of the first act invites a reader or spectator to think analogically (to consider how one problem is like or unlike another). It introduces a play where the solution to any one problem depends upon a solution to all the others. Similarly schematic first acts can be found in *Measure for Measure* (which I have discussed in section C of Chapter Five); and in *Troilus and Cressida*, where the first scene shows us Troilus disputing with Pandarus about the fairness of Cressida, the second shows us Cressida disputing with Pandarus about the fairness of Troilus, and the third shows us the Greek generals disputing with each other about the virtues of Achilles – only to be interrupted by the Trojan Aeneas bringing a challenge on behalf of Hector, who claims that he 'hath a lady wiser, fairer, truer, / Than ever Greek did compass in his arms' (1.3.275–6).

B.

Not all Shakespearean first acts are as systematic and orderly as the three discussed above. Most, in fact, are not, even when they do the necessary work of introducing the play's main characters, conflicts and themes. At the end of the first act of *Merchant* we can already anticipate that Bassanio will find that the success of his romance might mean the death of his friend. By contrast, at the end of the first act of *Richard II*, we might guess (or, if we are familiar with English history, know) that the banishment of Bolingbroke will be the downfall of Richard. The structure of *Richard II*'s first act does not, however, invite us to see this ironic reversal as the most important thing about the action; rather, it asks us to consider the difference between how powerful men speak in public and how they speak in private. The first and third scenes show us the elaborate preparations for, and the surprising avoidance of, the highly public spectacle of a judicial combat: Henry Bolingbroke has challenged Thomas Mowbray to a duel to avenge the murder of Bolingbroke's uncle, Thomas of Woodstock, the Duke of Gloucester – a murder that King Richard II himself probably ordered. Much of the drama of these scenes lies in listening to the king, Bolingbroke, Mowbray and Bolingbroke's father John of Gaunt speak about Gloucester's death, and who was responsible for it, in heavily coded terms: no one can safely accuse Richard.

In the second scene, on the other hand, John of Gaunt speaks to the widowed Duchess of Gloucester and, in asking her to understand that her husband's murder might never be avenged, speaks more frankly (if still quite circumspectly) of Richard's role in the murder:

> God's is the quarrel, for God's substitute,
> His deputy anointed in His sight,
> Hath caused his death, the which if wrongfully,

> Let heaven revenge, for I may never lift
> An angry arm against His minister.
>
> (1.2.37–41)

In the fourth scene, we do not see Richard acknowledging responsibility for the death of Gloucester, but we do see him surrounded by flattering friends and crowing about the banishment of Bolingbroke and the imminent death of Gaunt. 'Old John of Gaunt is grievous sick,' says Bushy (1.4.54), recalling the first line of the play, spoken by King Richard: 'Old John of Gaunt, time honoured Lancaster'. Richard's response, the last lines of 1.4, are somewhat less solemn: 'Come, gentlemen, let's all go visit him. / Pray God we may make haste, and come too late!' (63–4). The first act as a whole, then, is not a précis of the play's action so much as an invitation to begin thinking a certain way: alternating scenes allow us to set characters' public words against their private, and thus establish a baseline for judging political speech throughout the play. One of the most interesting things that happens over the next four acts is that Shakespeare closes the gap between Richard's public and private speech but widens the gap for Bolingbroke.

The first act of *Richard II*, where alternating scenes create a sense of naturally unfolding action, even as similarities between them create a particular perspective from which to view it, represents Shakespeare's most typical approach to first-act construction. We see this approach as well in the first act of *King Lear*, whose five scenes offer for our analysis a surprisingly wide range of father–child and king–subject relationships; and in the first act of *Macbeth*, where six scenes of Macbeth being talked about (sometimes when he is present) by virtually all the other characters in the play are followed by a seventh that begins with Macbeth alone, contemplating regicide in a long soliloquy. A variation on this multi-perspectival form can be seen in the first acts of *The Comedy of Errors, Romeo and Juliet* and *Othello*, where implicit and explicit connections between the scenes of the first act imply a kind of action, and resolution of the action, that is very different from what actually happens in the play. The sense of naturally unfolding action arises in part from the fact that the expectations created by the first act are thwarted by the action of subsequent acts. I will focus only on *The Comedy of Errors* in the discussion that follows.

C.

In the first scene of *The Comedy of Errors*, the Duke of Ephesus tells Egeon that the only way to avoid the death penalty, having landed illegally at Ephesus, is to pay a fine of 'a thousand marks' (1.1.21). Egeon does not have the money, but the duke gives him the whole day to

> seek thy hope by beneficial help.
> Try all the friends thou hast in Ephesus,
> Beg thou or borrow to make up the sum,
> And live. If no, then thou art doomed to die.
>
> (1.1.151–4)

In the very next scene, we meet Egeon's son, Antipholus of Syracuse, who has also (unbeknownst to his father) recently and illegally landed at Ephesus, and who is planning to spend an hour or so sight-seeing: 'I will go lose myself / And wander up and down to view the city' (1.2.30–1). Before he does this, he gives his slave Dromio a bag of money to deposit at their inn for safe-keeping. At 1.2.81, when Antipholus of Syracuse mistakes Dromio of Ephesus for his own slave, we learn the exact amount contained in the bag of money: it is a 'thousand marks'. The pieces of a comic plot have been carefully put in place: Egeon and his son, both wandering around an unfamiliar city, neither aware of the other's presence nor of the Ephesian twins, will repeatedly cross paths, and are likely to interact without recognizing one another; at the end of the play, somehow, the thousand marks Antipholus of Syracuse has given to Dromio will end up being used to pay Egeon's ransom. And yet, of course, the plot that unfolds from the first act is nothing like this: Egeon does not appear again until the final scene; in that scene, it is Antipholus of Ephesus, not Antipholus of Syracuse, who offers to ransom his father (and with a different bag of money); and the Duke of Ephesus is content to release Egeon without collecting the fine.

Like the first words, then, the first act of a Shakespeare play sounds a keynote, anticipates or encapsulates later action and themes, and creates expectations (not all of which are necessarily fulfilled) about the action to follow. In reading the first act closely, however, it is important to remember that, while a reader can see, on the page, where the second act starts, a spectator is very unlikely to know when one act ends and another begins. Sometimes (as will be discussed further below) the second act will involve a change of location or subject: in the second act of *Othello*, for example, the action moves from Venice to Cyprus, and in the second act of *Romeo and Juliet* (which is, like the first, preceded by a chorus) Rosaline has been replaced by Juliet as the object of Romeo's affection. But not all plays are so orderly. The first three scenes of *Coriolanus* alternate between Rome and Corioles, and their subject is preparations for war between the two states; the next seven scenes dramatize the war. It would be easy to feel, sitting in the theatre, that the first war scene was the beginning of the second act, especially because that scene follows a domestic scene in Rome where Caius Martius's wife, mother and mother's friend talk about the great soldier; but in fact, the first ten scenes of this play make up the first act. On the other hand, the first scene of the second act of *Richard II*, which opens with a private conversation between Gaunt and his brother York, fits into the alternating scene pattern I described above; because of this, and because 2.1 ends with Gaunt's death, it might feel more like the end of the first act than the beginning of the second. Finally, and in the same vein, the first act of *A Midsummer Night's Dream* is only two scenes long, with one introducing the aristocratic lovers (not only the Athenian youths but also Theseus and Hippolyta), and the other introducing the working-class men who will perform a love tragedy for the wedding celebration that ends the play. Unlike *The Merchant of Venice*, which introduces all three of its distinct spaces or spheres in the first act, *Dream* introduces only two, deferring the introduction of the supernatural characters until the first scene of Act 2. Of course, a spectator in the theatre might reasonably assume that this scene, which begins with Puck, Oberon and Titania, is the third scene of Act 1.

Conclusion

As noted in Chapter Three, no Shakespeare play printed during the playwright's lifetime records act *or* scene breaks on the page, and the act divisions given in the 1623 Folio texts cannot with certainty be treated as authorial. Shakespeare is likely to have thought of five-act structure as conventional, but here as in every other element of his dramatic and poetic art, his primary interest seems to be in the arbitrarinesss or permeability of boundaries between any one thing and another. The act divisions that editors have put in modern texts, usually (though not in every case) following those given in the Folio, are reliable and useful guides for reading closely the architecture of a play. They help you to see the rigorous, ornate, often syncopated way in which Shakespeare coordinates the relation between part and whole. But they are also artificial and misleading markers of organization; they can tell you more about how Shakespeare constructed the play than about how an audience or reader actually experiences it, which is as a scene-by-scene (perhaps even an entrance-by-entrance) unfolding, where the final shape of the always mutable whole is never in view until after the play ends.

CHAPTER SEVEN

The Third Act

Overview

The third act is the centre of the play, in both expository and thematic terms. This chapter provides different ways of reading Act 3 closely. In section A, I focus on the first scene of the act, especially when that scene dramatizes something that seems unrelated to the main action. In section B, I discuss Shakespeare's tendency to put into the third act moments that epitomize the play's central concerns. In section C, I discuss how the third act functions as a turning point between the two halves of a play.

A.

If you want to get a vivid sense of both what a Shakespeare play is and what it is not, a good place to look is the third act, and especially the first scene of the third act. As I have already begun to suggest in my analysis of the Ventidius scene in *Antony and Cleopatra* (see Chapter Three, section B), the first scene of the third act can provide a perspective on the main action of the play by taking the reader or spectator far away from that action and introducing an entirely new (and usually transitory) verbal idiom.

Antony and Cleopatra 3.1 suggests that there is a place in the world where the virtues lacking in the title characters might still exist. The title characters seem oblivious to the existence of such a place, and the reader or spectator is given very little time or context within which to make sense of it in relation to the main action, but we are, at least, provided with a glimpse. The first scene of the third act in *The Winter's Tale* performs a similar function. Here, Cleomenes and Dion, sent by Leontes to consult the oracle at Delphos about Hermione's fidelity, discuss their trip:

CLEOMENES
The climate's delicate, the air most sweet,
Fertile the isle, the temple much surpassing
The common praise it bears.

(3.1.1–3)

These lines make it sound as if the characters are in Delphi, at the temple of the oracle: perhaps, we might think, we are about to see the ceremony of consultation itself. The next lines, however, shift into the past tense and indicate that the ceremony has already happened.

DION I shall report,
For most it caught me, the celestial habits –
Methinks I so should term them – and the reverence
Of the grave wearers. O, the sacrifice,
How ceremonious, solemn and unearthly
It was i'th' offering!
CLEOMENES But of all, the burst
And the ear-deafening voice o'th' oracle,
Kin to Jove's thunder, so surprised my sense
That I was nothing.

(3–11)

Especially after the violent jealousy, terrible accusations and suggestively ambiguous evidence (the fact, for example, that Hermione was nine months pregnant at the end of Polixenes' nine-month visit) of the previous two acts, this, the awesome ceremony of truth being handed down from on high, would have been something to see. It is, however, kept offstage, and, what is more, Cleomenes and Dion do not themselves know what judgement the oracle has rendered.

DION

If th'event o'th' journey
Prove as successful to the queen – O, be't so –
As it hath been to us rare, pleasant, speedy,
The time is worth the use on't.

(11–14)

All they, and we, have to go on, in assessing what the truth is likely to be, is the delightful experience of having been out of claustrophobic Sicilia, enjoying the delicate climate and the beautiful people of the holy isle. When they return to Sicily, the truth they long to hear will be revealed, but it will also be completely disregarded by Leontes. The first scene of the third act provides Cleomenes and Dion with a glimpse – and the reader or spectator with the report of a glimpse – of a place in the world where truth can be known, and where it is revered. Whether the truth revealed in such a place has any reality in the world of the play remains an open question: although Leontes is, in 3.2, convinced of the oracle's truth, it is only because of the sudden death of his son and (apparently) his wife precipitated by his rash denial.

The first scene of the third act in *Othello* offers a perspective on the main action in a different way. The miserable Cassio, hoping to atone for his violent drunkenness the night before, pays musicians to play a song beneath Othello's window wishing him and his bride good morning. His musicians are sent away by an insolent clown who is adept at wordplay in a way that directly recalls Iago:

CASSIO

Dost thou hear, mine honest friend?

CLOWN

No, I hear not your honest friend, I hear you.

(3.1.21–2)

The clown will reappear once more in 3.4, now quibbling with Desdemona, and again recalling Iago:

DESDEMONA

Do you know, sirrah, where lieutenant Cassio lies?

CLOWN
I dare not say he lies anywhere.
DESDEMONA
Why, man?
CLOWN
He's a soldier and for me to say a soldier lies, 'tis stabbing.
(3.4.1–6)

In these moments, the play seems on the verge of becoming the play that its plot always suggests it might be: a comedy in which an older man marries a younger woman and is understandably consumed with fear that she will be seduced by other men; he and the good friend he most suspects with his wife are both humiliated by their own bad behaviour and, ultimately, the husband's jealousy is proved to be groundless. The echoes of Iago in the clown's wordplay both make that wordplay more sinister than it might seem in a more comic play and emphasize how simple the tricks are by which Iago manages to turn Othello's jealousy into violence. *Othello* 3.1 is different from *Antony and Cleopatra* 3.1 and *Winter's Tale* 3.1 in that it does not provide a glimpse of an alternative to the problems of the main action so much as it recapitulates those problems in a different register.

B.

While the first scene of the third act often takes a reader or spectator far outside the main action, the third act as a whole often contains an elaborate theatrical or metaphorical gesture that seems to sum up the play's largest thematic and expository concerns. Sometimes 3.1 does both things at once: in *Troilus and Cressida*, for example, 3.1 is the scene in which Helen of Troy makes her only appearance. With the same satirical audacity that characterizes the entire play, Shakespeare gives us a Helen who is a mere shadow of her mythical self, with little more to do in this scene than insist that Pandarus sing a vacuous love song – which peters out inarticulately: 'Love, love, nothing but love, still love still more / … / "O! O!" groans out for "Ha, ha, ha!" – Heigh-ho!' (3.1.109–21). Helen's own vacuous, repetitive lines (e.g. 'My lord Pandarus, honey-sweet lord – ', 63;

'Let thy song be love. "This love will undo us all." O Cupid, Cupid, Cupid!' 104–5) make it difficult to see her as the 'theme of honour and renown' (2.2.199) that might justify the deadlocked Trojan war. At least for the space of this scene she seems to be an all-too-human woman, rather mindlessly consumed with trivial desire, and the fact that she does not appear outside this scene suggests that neither she nor the Greek and Trojan warriors have any idea what the war is really about. *Troilus and Cressida* 3.1 provides a stark perspective on the main action and, simultaneously, encapsulates the intractable problems of the main action.

More commonly, emblematic scenes or theatrical gestures in the third act occur outside the first scene. Here is a partial list of third-act gestures that seem to sum up in vivid terms what the entire play is about: King Lear rages in the storm; Hamlet speaks his 'To be or not to be' speech and stages his 'Mousetrap' play; the ghost of Banquo confronts Macbeth at his coronation banquet; in *1 Henry IV*, the rebels Hotspur and Mortimer, together with their Welsh ally Glendower, divide a map of England into three parts, envisioning the new political order that will emerge from their war against Henry IV; in *Measure for Measure*, Isabella and the disguised duke concoct the ingenious bed-trick plot by means of which they will circumvent Angelo's coercive demands; and in *The Merry Wives of Windsor*, Sir John Falstaff, pursuing an adulterous liaison, hides in a laundry basket and is thrown into the river Thames together with the dirty laundry piled on top of him.

Of course, the third act is not the only place where such emblematic gestures occur: the Mechanicals' performance of *Pyramus and Thisbe*, for example, occurs in the fifth act of *A Midsummer Night's Dream*. And it is in the fourth act of *Cymbeline* that Innogen mistakes Cloten's beheaded body for the body of her lover Posthumus – a moment that makes explicit the disconcerting comparison the play has been inviting us to draw between two apparently opposite characters. I think that emblematic gestures such as those I have described probably occur most frequently in the third act, but whether or not that is the case, what is distinctive about those I have described is their third-act position: they are not so much the consequence of, as reflections upon, the action that has preceded them, and further action follows from them.

Its thematic significance notwithstanding, Innogen's mistaking of Cloten's body for Posthumus's is an accident brought about by a chain of circumstance that Shakespeare has been linking together almost since the first scene of the play; it can only happen when it happens, and once it happens, it is inconsequential. By contrast, the meeting between Cymbeline and the Roman ambassador could happen at virtually any time in the first half of the play; Shakespeare puts it in the third act (indeed, the first scene of the third act) not only because it is a consequential meeting, precipitating the complex action that the fourth and fifth acts must unwind, but also because (as discussed in Chapter One, section B) the conflict it represents between Italy and Britain, submission and resistance, is the expository and thematic heart of the play.

C.

Because it both draws together the diverse strands of the action of the first two acts and sets the play on a course for new, climactic action in the final two acts, the third act is often very busy. In the third act of *Richard II*, we see Bolingbroke, recently returned to England, demonstrate his newly consolidated power by arraigning Richard's loyal followers Bushy and Green; we see Richard return (too late!) to England from Ireland and face wave upon wave of bad news about the progress of Bolingbroke's rebellion; and we see the meeting between Bolingbroke and Richard, mediated by Northumberland, which sets the stage not only for Richard's deposition but for many years of civil war. In the third act of *Othello*, Cassio asks Emilia to solicit Desdemona on his behalf, Desdemona and Cassio are seen speaking together by Othello and Iago, Iago begins to make Othello jealous of Cassio, Desdemona drops her handkerchief, Emilia gives the handkerchief to Iago, Iago convinces Othello of Desdemona's infidelity, Othello confronts Desdemona about the handkerchief, and Cassio, having found the handkerchief, gives it to Bianca. The busyness is sometimes offset by a moment of rhythmic variation, as in *Othello* 3.2, where Othello and two gentlemen of Cyprus go to view some fortifications – the one and only time in the play where we are able to see the general doing the work of a general; or as in *Richard II* 3.4, where the queen overhears the gardeners elaborately unfolding a metaphor of the kingdom as a garden. But just as often, and especially in comedies, the third act, the act of crisis, is unrelentingly busy.

With two acts on either side, the third act is literally a turning point. That is one reason it makes sense for its first scene to take the reader or speaker beyond the geographical or tonal realm of the main action: we are able at this moment to see just how much the play contains, or might contain, and to feel a sense of excitement and possibility about all the directions the action might still take. The first scene of Act 3 can serve this purpose even while remaining anchored in the world of the main action. In *The Comedy of Errors* 3.1, the Syracusan twins are inside Antipholus of Ephesus's house while the Ephesian twins are locked out; the door separating them, always in danger of being forced open by Antipholus of Ephesus, narrowly averts the family reunion – and, perhaps, the redirection of the plot into a search for Egeon by his children. *Romeo and Juliet* 3.1 is the scene where both Tybalt and Mercutio die, turning what has been a conventional comic plot (two young lovers work to outsmart their overbearing parents, enlisting the help of a bawdy nurse and an indulgent friar) into a tragedy (the lovers' plans are swallowed up in the violence of the family feud). When the wounded Mercutio upbraids Romeo for coming between him and Tybalt – 'I was hurt under your arm' (3.1.105) – Romeo's reply is heart-breaking because it is both entirely sincere and entirely reasonable: 'I thought all for the best' (106). He had no way of knowing that he was an actor in a tragedy. Of course the dramatization of multiple possibilities is not limited to the first scene of the act: *Hamlet* 3.3 shows us Hamlet with his sword poised over the neck of the praying Claudius, and 3.4 ends with the prince suggesting cryptically that he has plans to deal with the 'bloat King' (3.4.180) as well as Rosencrantz and Guildenstern, whom he trusts no more than 'adders fanged' (201). The third act of *King Lear* ends with the blinded Gloucester being thrust out of his house. The end of the third act generally sends us, and the characters, at breakneck speed into some complex, unforeseen action.

Conclusion

The third act allows us to see that any Shakespeare play contains within itself other possible plays. A good example with which to conclude is *3 Henry VI*, whose third act, the turning point in the civil war between Henry VI and Edward IV, is typically action-packed: Henry, hiding out in a forest, is arrested by Edward's gamekeepers; King Edward woos the widow Elizabeth Grey; the Earl of Warwick, unaware of Edward's current romantic interest, travels to France on his earlier instructions and proposes that Edward marry King Lewis XI's daughter Bona; this embassy, and Lewis's assent to the proposal, are interrupted and superseded by the arrival of a post from England announcing Edward's marriage to Elizabeth Grey; Lewis then sends an army of 5,000 soldiers with Warwick and the Earl of Oxford to fight Edward. The act also contains something typically unexpected, a forceful theatrical gesture that takes us, in a new register and idiom, away from the concerns of the main action: this is Richard Duke of Gloucester's 72-line speech (3.2.124–95) expressing his desire to 'catch the English crown' (179) and his willingness to 'frame my face to all occasions' (185) to satisfy this desire. Although Shakespeare's first audiences would have been aware that Richard Gloucester would go on to become King Richard III, the character has been a minor part up to this point, and the text contains no hint that Gloucester's ambitions will become the subject of the drama. Indeed, even after this speech, Gloucester's ambitions do *not* become the subject of the drama – there is still too much for the play to cover in Edward's march to power – though it does come to the surface briefly in 4.1 and throughout the penultimate scene, 5.6, where Gloucester murders Henry VI. The gesture made by Gloucester in 3.2 is not simply to another space within the world of the play, but rather to another play altogether: to *Richard III*, which Shakespeare may well have been writing at the same time he was writing *3 Henry VI* – or which, perhaps, he *decided* to write as he wrote this speech. In *3 Henry VI* 3.2, Shakespeare makes Gloucester much more important than he needs to be; in so doing, he suggests both that Gloucester's all-consuming ambition epitomizes the forces underlying the sprawling civil war to which he has devoted three plays, and that the current play must become something else if it is to explain those forces fully.

CHAPTER EIGHT

The Second and Fourth Acts

Overview

If the first and third acts drive the action of the play, the second and fourth provide new perspectives on that action. In this chapter I begin with *The Taming of the Shrew*, which, because it is one of Shakespeare's more narrowly focused plays, provides good examples of what the second and fourth acts do in most plays in the Shakespeare canon. The second act twines two strands of action together, often while developing a dynamic contrast: in *Shrew* it is a contrast between speed and dilation. The fourth act, on the other hand, broadens the perspective on the main action by introducing new characters (many of whom do not appear again), and by folding formerly peripheral characters into the main action's central problems. Some variations on these general principles are described in sections B and C of this chapter, which focus on *Henry V* and *Titus Andronicus* respectively.

A.

The first two acts of *The Taming of the Shrew* set in motion two marriage plots, each moving at a different pace. They start out in parallel. The first act introduces Lucentio in the first scene and Petruccio in the second. Both men are strangers to Padua, and each falls into his wooing plot by chance: Lucentio has come to Padua as a tourist and catches sight of Bianca in the street as her father Baptista speaks with a number of her suitors; Petruccio is travelling specifically to find a wife, and decides to pursue Katherine after his friend Hortensio jestingly raises the possibility. The second act is a single long scene where all the suitors of both Katherine and Bianca come to speak with Baptista. Here, Petruccio rapidly makes a deal with Baptista for Katherine's hand and then, after a brisk conversation with the bride-to-be herself, informs her that, 'will you, nill you, I will marry you' (2.1.273). The main dramatic point here is the speed of the wooing: 'Was ever match clapped up so suddenly?' says the awed Gremio (329). By contrast, Lucentio's wooing of Bianca unfolds in a comically dilatory fashion: Lucentio disguises himself as a schoolmaster in order to woo Bianca while his servant Tranio, disguised as Lucentio, conducts marriage negotiations with Baptista. The second act, then, both extends in a linear fashion the two plot strands from the first and establishes a contrast between two types, and speeds, of wooing. The contrasts culminate in the play's final scene when, at the banquet celebrating Lucentio's wedding, Katherine submits to Petruccio in elaborate, public fashion while Bianca proves to be a headstrong wife.

Act 4 is also built around a contrast between the two couples: Petruccio begins 'solving' the problems of his marriage (depriving Katherine of food and sleep, offering and then taking away beautiful clothes, forcing her to call the sun the moon) while Lucentio pursues an increasingly complex course (enlisting a stranger to impersonate his father, arranging to marry Bianca behind her father's back) on the way to his. These actions unfold, mostly predictably, from the two climactic scenes in Act 3: in the first, the disguised Lucentio and his rival Hortensio (himself disguised as a music-master) discover themselves to Bianca, who betrays little about where her affections lie and leaves the men in suspense as she goes to prepare for her sister's wedding; in the second, Katherine and Petruccio are married. But the focus of Act 4 is less narrowly on the two couples than it has been. The five scenes of this act introduce a wide range of minor characters: Petruccio's servants Curtis, Nathaniel, Philip, Joseph and Nicholas (4.1); the travelling pedant who agrees to disguise himself as Vincentio (4.2 and 4.4); a haberdasher and a tailor (4.3); and Lucentio's father Vincentio (4.5). Drawn unwittingly into the violence of Petruccio's romance, or the elaborate complexity of Lucentio's, these characters allow us to see the similarity between the two marriage plots: each depends upon the willingness of the lovers to treat identity – their own or that of others – as something that can be changed (and changed back again) at a moment's notice.

Act 4 also makes the previously introduced characters Grumio and Hortensio important in new ways: Grumio's attitude towards Petruccio's violent manner, both in the scene he has alone with the other servants (4.1.1–105) and in the scene where he assists with the taming (4.3), gives a reader or spectator one way of measuring the cruelty with which Petruccio treats his new wife. Does Grumio, an oft-beaten servant who readily imitates his master when he speaks with inferior servants (see 4.1.1–10 and 50–60), take pleasure in depriving Katherine of food (see 4.3.20–30), or should we understand from his first line in 4.3, 'No, no, forsooth, I dare not for my life', that he withholds food mainly because he fears Petruccio as much as she does? Hortensio, meanwhile, having been bested by Lucentio in the competition for Bianca, announces that he will turn his attentions to a 'wealthy widow' who 'hath as long loved me' as he has loved Bianca (4.2.38–9). This unexpected turn of events is followed by Hortensio's equally unexpected presence at Petruccio's house during the taming. His reaction to what he sees is as important as Grumio's, and rather more explicit: after observing Petruccio's forceful way with Katherine in 4.3 and 4.5, Hortensio declares himself ready to encounter the widow, even 'if she be froward' (4.5.77). Thus, although we hear nothing about this widow prior to 4.2, and we do not see her until the final scene, her marriage to Hortensio can be presented in parallel to the other two marriages in the final scene.

B.

The first and second acts of *Henry V* are extremely efficient in their representation of Henry V's decision to invade France and take possession of the throne he believes rightfully to be his: in 1.1, we see the English clergy decide, for self-interested reasons, to throw its support behind Henry's claim to the French throne; in 1.2, the Archbishop of Canterbury justifies that claim and Henry meets with an ambassador from France who defies it; in 2.2, Henry discovers and punishes a French-backed conspiracy of English lords against his life and then prepares to sail for France; and in 2.4 the French king and his son discuss the imminent invasion and meet with the

English ambassador, who once more presses Henry's claim. In just four short scenes across two acts the stage is set for the war that will take up all of Acts 3 and 4. The contrast could not be plainer with the opening scenes and acts of the two *Henry IV* plays, where both Henry IV and Prince Hal are unable or unwilling to move forward in causes of great urgency. In the structure of *Henry V*'s opening action we can see that the new king has left his old self behind.

And yet, the second act of *Henry V* does not let us forget about Prince Hal entirely. The first scene of Act 2 brings onstage Hal's old tavern-mates – Bardolph, Pistol, Mistress Quickly, as well as a new character named Nym – whose concern with the upcoming French war is secondary to the rivalry between Nym and Pistol for the hand of Mistress Quickly. Pistol has married her, and the two men exchange violent words:

> NYM
> I have an humour to knock you indifferently well. If you grow foul with me, Pistol, I will scour you with my rapier, as I may, in fair terms. If you would walk off, I would prick your guts a little, in good terms, as I may, that's the humour of it.
> PISTOL
> O braggart vile and damned furious wight,
> The grave doth gape, and doting death is near;
> Therefore exhale.
>
> (2.1.55–63)

The clear contrast here is with Henry and the French ambassador's parley in the previous scene, where rivalry (the 'mistress' is France) is expressed in more elevated terms.

> AMBASSADOR
> There's naught in France
> That can be with a nimble galliard won;
> You cannot revel into dukedoms there.
> [The dauphin] therefore sends you, meeter for your spirit,
> This tun of treasure; and in lieu of this,
> Desires you let the dukedoms that you claim
> Hear no more of you. This the dauphin speaks.

KING
What treasure, uncle?
EXETER
Tennis balls, my liege.
KING
We are glad the dauphin is so pleasant with us.
His present and your pains we thank you for.
When we have matched our rackets to these balls,
We will in France, by God's grace, play a set
Shall strike his father's crown into the hazard.
(1.2.252–64)

The dauphin's gift of tennis balls is intended to remind Henry of his misspent youth, and to suggest that he has not yet outlived it. The king's reply, though it acknowledges the joke, keeps its focus squarely on his present strength and future victory. The king refuses to admit that he is haunted by his past and, indeed, perhaps he is not. But the structure of the play suggests that he is (or ought to be), even if he doesn't know it; we see this not only in the lower-register echo made by Pistol and Nym's fight, but also in the second act's concern with Sir John Falstaff, who is said to be sick in 2.1 and whose death is reported in 2.3. 'The King has killed his heart,' Mistress Quickly says when talking of his illness (2.1.87). But after Falstaff is dead, there is no more looking backward: 'Shall we shog?' asks Nym, 'The King will be gone from Southampton' (2.3.43–4), and the tavern-haunters head off to the wars. The alternating structure of *Henry V*'s second act keeps the new king entangled with his past, and entangles those from his past with his march into the future.

The king's entanglement with his past is even greater in Act 4, though it is also presented much more subtly. This act covers the eve and the day of the battle of Agincourt, in which the English, facing long odds, rout the French; here, the king has numerous stirring speeches (4.1.147–84 and 222–81, 4.3.18–67 and 90–125, 4.8.81–113) in which he meditates candidly upon the awful power and responsibility of kingship or vaunts the courage and valour of the common English soldier. In this act, he is every inch a king, and the French appear, even to themselves, as frivolous amateurs: 4.2, where the French lords talk about how splendid their horses are and how badly the English are dressed, and 4.5, where they speak with almost comic affectation of their shameful defeat, are an inversion of the mockery in the 'tennis balls' scene. Yet even as Act 4 clearly demonstrates that Henry has come into his own as England's greatest king, its constantly shifting focus presents opportunities for a reader to feel that this is not the whole story. The battle of Agincourt itself takes up only three of the act's eight scenes (4.4, 4.5 and 4.6), and the only actual fighting that occurs onstage is between the cowardly Pistol and an unnamed French soldier, whose life Pistol spares for a ransom of two hundred crowns. Pistol is clearly meant to represent the opposite of the valiant common English soldier: the unnamed English boy who witnesses the encounter notes, in a moment that raises the specter of the king's past, that 'Bardolph and Nym had ten times more valour than this roaring devil ... and they are both hanged' (4.4.69–72). But to some extent Pistol acts more honourably than the king himself does in 4.6 when, hearing that the French have received reinforcements, he orders the English soldiers to kill the prisoners they were holding for ransom (4.6.32–8). There is something more than simple ironic contrast at work in Shakespeare's allowing the Pistol scene to represent the entire battle: in its representation of violent opportunism, its dramatization of English linguistic obtuseness (Pistol, like Henry with Princess Katherine later, requires an interpreter for his important transaction) and its reminder that Henry is a killer of friends whose worth he might not fully realize, 4.4 suggests that his kingship has not transcended the moral economy of thieves and braggarts.

Something similar is suggested by the action that gives structure to the act as a whole, namely the plot involving Michael Williams, whom Henry meets on the eve of the battle when he goes in disguise among his soldiers to hear what they think about him. This intelligence-gathering mission is a return to Henry's behaviour in the *Henry IV* plays, where the prince prided himself on his ability to speak the language of the common people, even as he watched for his moment to rise above their 'idleness' (*1 Henry IV* 1.2.189). This is not to suggest that 4.1 does not represent moments of genuine sympathy of the king for his subjects. Indeed, when Henry dons the cloak loaned to him by Sir Thomas Erpingham and goes among his men, the reader sees him as he would like to be seen: powerful because he is humble, compassionate because he is able to learn his subjects' secret thoughts. When he exchanges gages with Williams, and promises another time to make good the defence of the king he has offered against Williams's cynicism (4.1.197–214), we seem to be prepared for a scene later in the play where Williams will encounter Henry wearing the gage and the king can demonstrate majesty and clemency in a single moment. Such a scene does occur, but in a rather less straightforward way than we might expect. Henry does not confront Williams directly, but rather gives his gage to Fluellen to wear (4.7.149–54), with the result that Fluellen is challenged to fight – is indeed struck – by Williams (4.8.2–18) before the king intervenes and reveals that it was to himself that Williams spoke in 4.1. The elaborate prank is nowhere near as efficiently managed as the play's military action, and strongly recalls the young prince's involvement in the Gadshill robbery in *1 Henry IV* – where he wreaks havoc in the Kentish countryside simply for the pleasure of watching Falstaff tell self-aggrandizing lies. Fluellen, who, earlier in the act and with unwitting significance, compared Henry V to 'Alexander the Pig' because of his willingness to kill his best friend (see 4.6.11–52), learns that loyalty as much as disloyalty to this king comes at a cost.

C.

The first act of *Titus Andronicus* is one long scene that dramatizes political chaos in Rome. It begins with a competition between the brothers Bassianus and Saturninus for the empery; degenerates into violent fighting within Titus Andronicus's family after Titus is called upon to choose the emperor; and concludes with the chosen emperor, Saturninus, spurning the man who chose him and proposing to marry the captive Goth queen Tamora, who is secretly plotting her revenge. The second act dramatizes the violence that we might expect to arise from such chaos – though it is perhaps even more horrible than we might expect: the Goth queen's sons Chiron and Demetrius are given licence by their mother to wreak havoc within Rome; they murder Titus's son-in-law Bassianus and rape and mutilate his daughter Lavinia; two of Titus's other sons are falsely accused of, and imprisoned for, Bassianus's murder. As horrible as it is, the violence of the second act is represented in a much more organized way than the violence of the first act: it all revolves around and is managed by Aaron the Moor, a character who (as discussed in section B of Chapter Two) is a silent and ambiguous presence throughout most of the first act. It is Aaron who, in 2.1, suggests to Chiron and Demetrius that they might overcome their rivalry for the love of Lavinia by joining together to rape her; it is Aaron who, in 2.3, buries a bag of gold and a letter with which he will frame Titus's sons Quintus and Martius for the murder of Bassianus – and Aaron who tells Chiron and Demetrius where to deposit the body (see 2.2.185–6); and it is because of her fury at being mocked for loving Aaron that Tamora encourages her sons to rape Lavinia and 'make her sure' afterwards (2.2.187–91). When the mutilated Lavinia appears onstage in 2.3, it is certainly meant to be a shock – I think we probably expect that the brothers will simply kill her after the rape – but it is a somewhat different shock from the one Marcus Andronicus feels when he sees his niece. His speech at 2.3.11–57 dwells on a single question: who, what 'beast' (34), what 'monster' (44) did this? We know the answer that Lavinia is unable to speak and we know how the horrible event came about: we have followed the nightmarish logic of Aaron's plots from the first scene of the act. At the end of the first act of *Titus*, then, it is impossible to say who is in charge in Rome; at the end of the second act, we can be certain that it is Aaron.

Aaron remains in control throughout the third act, where we see the completion of his second-act plot – Quintus and Martius are executed, even after Titus cuts off his own hand as a ransom for their lives – but his role diminishes somewhat in the fourth act, which is mostly devoted to Titus's plotting. In 4.1 Titus finally learns the identity of his daughter's assailants, and begins to speak cryptically of revenge. He plans to send his grandson, young Lucius, armed with '[p]resents' for Tamora's sons (4.1.113–17) – these turn out to be 'a bundle of weapons, and verses writ upon them' (4.2.0 SD) – and then in 4.3, Titus and Marcus and young Lucius shoot arrows wrapped with messages into the emperor's palace. In this same scene, Titus waylays a passing clown (on his way 'to take up a matter of brawl betwixt my uncle and one of the emperal's men', 4.3.92–3) and asks him to deliver a 'supplication', wrapped around a knife, to Saturninus (102–21). It is unclear what all these messages are supposed to achieve: Titus, half-mad with grief, is not as meticulous a plotter as Aaron. The one act of violence Titus does effect in this act is unintended: when Saturninus reads the letter brought from Titus by the clown, he orders the clown to be summarily executed: 'Go take him away, and hang him presently'

(4.4.44). Titus's ineptitude in the fourth act stands in contrast to Aaron's efficiency in the second, and the contrast turns on the men's only direct encounter – when Aaron convinces Titus to cut off his own hand – in Act 3.

The contrast between Titus and Aaron dramatized in Act 4 depends in part upon the introduction of a new character, the clown. But the fourth act not only contrasts the two characters; it also provides a way of thinking about both of them as out of control of their own plotting, and it does so (again) in part by introducing a new character – the nurse. In 4.2, Chiron and Demetrius read, uncomprehendingly, the vengeful verses that young Lucius has just delivered. Aaron understands immediately that 'the old man hath found their guilt' (4.2.26). He holds this knowledge in reserve for the time being, and entertains himself and the empress's sons with indulgent thoughts of their unlikely triumph in Rome. It is at this moment of supreme complacency that Aaron, Chiron and Demetrius receive news from the nurse, who enters carrying a 'blackamoor child' (51 SD), that Tamora has given birth to a son. While Aaron certainly knows that he might be the father, he is also clearly in suspense (see 57–65); this is, perhaps, more even than he had dared hope for and he now must set about protecting his child's future. After suddenly, shockingly murdering the nurse, he announces to Chiron and Demetrius (in a revelation of new information that resembles the belated introduction of Hortensio's widow in *Shrew* Act 4) that the wife of a 'countryman' of his has 'but yesternight' given birth to a fair child; this child must stand in for the emperor's, while Aaron takes his own to be raised by the Goths (see 149–81). Aaron is not, like Titus, delusional, but he is, like Titus, improvising; and, as is the case with Titus, his improvisation draws characters who are totally unconnected to the main action into its terrible violence.

Conclusion

Aaron's hastily executed plan in Act 4 leads to his own downfall: he does not know that Titus's son Lucius has joined forces with the Goths, so he is captured by a Goth soldier as he is on his way to bring his child to a 'trusty Goth' (5.1.34). By contrast, while Titus's vengeful messages have little effect in Act 4, they do prompt Tamora to conceive a counterplot (see 4.4.96–113) in which she overplays her hand: imagining that Titus is more delusional than he actually is, she disguises herself and her two sons as Revenge, Rape and Murder, and arranges a meeting with Titus (in 5.2) which ultimately results in her sons' grisly murder. It would probably be inaccurate to say that Titus ends up better off than Aaron, but the shifting perspectives introduced by Act 4 create the necessary conditions for oppositions to give way to likeness in Act 5: both are fathers who have destroyed their families and themselves. We see something similar happen at the end of *Shrew*, where Lucentio confronts a shrewish wife at the same moment Petruccio presents a submissive one; and at the end of *Henry V* where the king's conquest of France is sealed in a wooing scene (5.2) whose main point is that the royal couple do not speak the same language. In each of the three plays discussed in this chapter, the broader perspective provided by the fourth act develops directly out of, or in response to, the structure of the second act; the second and fourth acts work together, and complement the work of the first and third, to make the fifth act's job – drawing all of the play's various expository and thematic strands together – extremely difficult.

CHAPTER NINE

The Last Act

Overview

I have tried to demonstrate in the foregoing chapters that Shakespeare's plays contain, or gesture towards, alternative versions of themselves. In the first act Shakespeare will often gesture towards actions that he does not pursue; in the second act, he will often introduce characters whose relationships and conflicts parallel those in the main action, of which they remain essentially unaware; in the first scene of Act 3, he will often shift to a location and an idiom far removed from that of the main action; and in the fourth act he will often introduce characters who have not appeared before and do not appear again. This is one way in which Shakespeare's plays come to feel so full of life, so driven by large and complex ideas: they imply that what you *do* see on the stage is only a fraction of what you *could* see.

The necessary purpose of the last act is to bring all, or most, of the strands of action together, and to give definition to the play as a whole by foreclosing various alternative possible actions. Even in the face of this formal necessity, Shakespeare works hard to maintain a feeling of diversity and possibility. In this chapter I describe some of the different ways Shakespeare approaches the task of ending his plays, and I focus on the tension in his last acts between a feeling of resolution or closure and a feeling of ongoing complication or possibility. In section A, I discuss some fifth acts that seem to ignore problems that have not been solved in the course of the action. In section B, I show that the fifth act will often introduce new problems for the characters (and the audience) to consider even as the problems of the preceding four acts are being solved. In section C, I discuss some emphatic but equivocal fifth-act resolutions; here, Shakespeare deliberately manipulates a reader's or spectator's expectations about when the play is over.

A.

The fifth act of *A Midsummer Night's Dream* brings all three of the play's groups of characters into the same location, Theseus's palace, and introduces these groups in the same order (nobles, mechanicals, fairies) in which they appeared at the beginning of the play. This symmetry, and the celebratory occasion with which the play ends, are meant to resolve the tensions and conflicts that have characterized the interactions within and between these groups in the preceding action, and to put all three groups into something like a harmonic relation. So the young lovers celebrate their nuptials simultaneously with Theseus and Hippolyta; the mechanicals perform a play in honour of the occasion; and the fairies bless the house, the marriages and the children that will come from them (5.1.393–400). Not least because of the mechanicals' performance of *Pyramus and Thisbe*, which lampoons the errors, misunderstandings and violent passions that have driven the action of the main play, the fifth act of *A Midsummer Night's Dream* is one of Shakespeare's most festive final acts.

Precisely because this act is so festive, and because it dramatizes that most ritualized of social occasions, a wedding celebration, its various minor tensions are puzzling, if not disturbing, once you notice them. Most notoriously, the young female lovers Hermia and Helena do not speak a word during the entire act. The silence of these women is in stark contrast to the volubility of their husbands, who join Theseus and Hippolyta in persistently interrupting the mechanicals as they blunder through their production of *Pyramus and Thisbe*. Not only is their speaking back to the play boorish in itself, it also contradicts the spirit of generosity in which Theseus proposed to take the performance just before it began.

Responding to Hippolyta's concern that the show will be terrible because, as Philostrate has just said, the actors 'can do nothing in this kind', Theseus says:

> Our sport shall be to take what they mistake.
> And what poor duty cannot do,
> Noble respect takes it in might, not merit.
> Where I have come, great clerks have purposed
> To greet me with premeditated welcomes
> Where I have seen them shiver and look pale,
> Make periods in the midst of sentences,
> Throttle their practised accent in their fears,
> And in conclusion dumbly have broke off,
> Not paying me a welcome. Trust me, sweet,
> Out of this silence yet I picked a welcome;
> And in the modesty of fearful duty
> I read as much as from the rattling tongue
> Of saucy and audacious eloquence.
>
> (5.1.89–103)

It is astonishing that, immediately after speaking this wonderfully humane speech, the duke can listen to Quince's nervously delivered prologue and then quip, 'This fellow doth not stand upon points' and 'His speech was like a tangled chain: nothing impaired, but all disordered' (5.1.118, 124–5). Are the mechanicals' feelings hurt, and is their performance even further impaired, by the heckling from their noble audience, or are they largely oblivious to what the spectators say? Is Theseus's plea for indulgence before the show merely disingenuous self-aggrandizement, or is he only gradually, reluctantly drawn into heckling the play because it amuses his new wife and he is eager to keep up with the wit of Demetrius and Lysander? Are Helena and Hermia silent because they find their new husbands surprisingly unpleasant, or are they simply laughing too hard to speak? Are the young lovers united in festivity and laughter, or do they find, now that they've got what they want, that they simply don't have much to say to each other? These seem like obvious questions to ask, and urgent ones to answer, if you read the play closely, but it is also the case that thinking about them at all seems at odds with the final act's festive spirit. It is hard to be certain whether Shakespeare is trying to raise these questions through the structure of the scene, or whether they simply arise incidentally as he moves the play, with as much laughter and festivity as possible, towards its resolution.

A similar ambiguity attends upon the strangely unresolved state of Demetrius and Helena's marriage at the end of the play. At the beginning of the play, both Demetrius and Lysander are in love with Hermia. In 2.2, Puck mistakenly squeezes the flower-juice on Lysander's eyes, causing him to fall in love with Helena; in 3.2, Puck partially corrects his mistake by squeezing the flower-juice on Demetrius's eyes, causing him to fall in love with Helena as well. At the end of 3.2, Puck draws the four confused and feuding lovers to the same place and causes them to sleep; he then puts a 'remedy' on Lysander's eye, so that when he wakes up he will take 'True delight / In the sight / Of thy former lady's eye' (3.2.455–7). Puck does not seem to do anything to Demetrius at this point and, indeed, if he were to cause Demetrius to take delight in his 'former lady's eye', it would only rekindle the play's conflicts, for Demetrius would once again be in love with Hermia. Because of how Shakespeare has set up the conflict between the young lovers, the resolution promised by Puck – 'Jack shall have Jill, / Nought shall go ill' (461–2) – seems to depend upon Demetrius remaining under the influence of the magical flower, compelled to love a woman whom, earlier in the play, he had viciously rebuked: 'Tempt not too much the hatred of my spirit; / For I am sick when I do look on thee' (2.1.211–12). As with Theseus's strange and rapid change of attitude towards the mechanicals, and as with the young women's silence at the wedding, it is possible not to notice that Demetrius and Helena are in a rather different position from Lysander and Hermia, and if we do notice, we might imagine that it is simply an oversight on Shakespeare's part, or a problem that is incidental but not integral to the structure of the play.

Shakespeare's fifth acts often seem to introduce tensions that they then ignore, or treat unresolved complications from earlier in the play as though they have been resolved. In *Titus Andronicus*, to take an example from the opposite end of the generic spectrum, the fate of Aaron's child, a crucial plot point in 5.1 – Lucius agrees to 'nurse and bring him up' in exchange for Aaron's confession of his villainy (5.1.73–85) – remains somewhat ambiguous in 5.3. The baby is brought onstage with Lucius after Titus's bloody banquet ('Behold the child,' Marcus says at 5.3.118–26, 'The issue of an irreligious Moor'), but Lucius does not mention the promise he made to Aaron, and after Marcus's lines no one, not even Aaron (brought onstage around line 175), mentions the child again. The final scene is intensely focused on children: Titus serves Tamora's sons to her in a pie and then kills his own daughter; Lucius avenges the murder of his father Titus by killing Saturninus (5.3.65–6); Lucius's son, Young Lucius, speaks a lament for the death of Titus Andronicus (172–5); and Aaron, promising the Romans that the cruel death they have devised for him will serve no moral purpose, says 'I am no baby, I, that with base prayers / I should repent the evils I have done' (184–5). To attend to the fate of Aaron's baby would seem to be essential to the scene, and it is remarkable that even the word 'baby' in Aaron's line does not cause the matter to be taken up. Perhaps Shakespeare and his actors had a definite idea of what should be done with, and how the actors onstage would telegraph their intentions for, the small prop representing this baby, and so the playwright did not feel the need to record these things in the text; in any case, the text offers no hint. Whether Lucius ever meant to or could possibly honour his promise to Aaron, and whether Rome will now be ruled by another man who slaughters children, are to some extent open questions, and to some extent questions the scene does not even ask.

B.

When Lucius makes his promise to Aaron and then returns to Rome in the last act of *Titus Andronicus*, it is as the head of an army of Goths: he had fled Rome at the end of 3.1, advised by his father to 'raise an army' among the Goths, and with them to be 'revenged on Rome and Saturnine' (3.1.286, 301). At the beginning of 5.1, preparing his invasion, he exhorts the Goth lords to

> be as your titles witness,
> Imperious, and impatient of your wrongs,
> And wherein Rome hath done you any scath
> Let him make treble satisfaction.
>
> (5–8)

As so often in Shakespeare, the end of the play is a variation on the beginning: returning to Rome, a warrior surnamed Andronicus lets in an enemy force that is given licence to takes its revenge upon Romans. It may well be that things will work out differently for Lucius; perhaps his alliance with the Goths, together with his promise to Aaron, are a sign of his awareness that Rome, if it is to survive, must assimilate rather than simply attempt to destroy the external forces that encroach upon it. It is equally possible, especially given the lines he speaks to end the play ('[Tamora's] life was beastly and devoid of pity / And being dead, let birds on her take pity', 5.3.198–9), that Lucius has learned nothing from the violence he has lived through, that he will perpetuate the cycle of slaughter and vengeance, and that the Rome he hopes to 'heal' (5.3.147) will suffer from the violence he cannot stop. In its unsettling symmetry with the first act, the last act of *Titus Andronicus* is a subtle and potent example of Shakespeare's tendency to introduce, at the end of his plays, new and potentially intractable problems – the material for an entirely new play, or the same play all over again with different characters – even as he works to bring together and solve the problems of all the strands of the main action.

A more explicit example can be found in the final act of *All's Well That Ends Well*. The first two scenes of this act lay the foundation for Bertram's humiliation: in one scene we see Helena and Diana return to France – in search of the king, who has removed to Rossillion – and in another we see Parolles return to Rossillion, now a penitent supplicant to Lavatch and Lafew. These two scenes are very carefully put in parallel: in 5.1, Helena gives a 'paper' (31) to a servant, asking that it be delivered to the king himself – this will turn out to be, in 5.3, a supplication by Diana for justice in her alleged affair with Bertram. In 5.2, Parolles presents a 'paper' (15) to Lavatch, asking that it be presented to Lafew so that Parolles might be taken back into the countess's household. It is clear that Helena's paper is meant to be worth more than Parolles's, which Lavatch considers as a piece of toilet paper (5.2.16–17), but the parallel between the scenes is also meant to suggest that both characters are fully complicit in Bertram's follies even as they try to separate themselves from them. These two scenes nicely pave the way, then, for the play's final scene, which demonstrates that it is not as easy as all that to humiliate Bertram.

In 5.3, after Helena and Bertram are reconciled, the King of France offers to reward the Florentine maid Diana for her part in the plot by means of which Helena brought Bertram to heel:

If thou beest yet a fresh uncropped flower
Choose thou thy husband and I'll pay thy dower.

(5.3.321–2)

This is exactly the reward the king earlier promised Helena for curing his disease – that is, it is the proposition that precipitated virtually all the complications that the fifth act has seemed to solve. The king's 'If' at the beginning of his proposition even echoes Bertram's 'If' a few lines earlier when he rather circumspectly accepts Helena's claim that she has fulfilled the terms of the letter he sent after he abandoned her:

If she, my liege, can make me know this clearly
I'll love her dearly, ever, ever dearly.

(309–10)

The parallel 'If's are a quiet reminder of how much must still be verified and brought to light before the play's complications can be considered resolved. Even if the bed-trick is explained to the king's satisfaction, Diana remains the mere daughter of an inn-keeper, and no more suitable a match for a courtier than Helena, the doctor's daughter, was. And even if Bertram accepts that Helena really has fulfilled the terms of his letter (it is worth noting that she does not precisely quote the letter, but rather glosses over Bertram's demand that she show him 'a child begotten of [her] body'), it is hard to imagine how he will ever rest easy in the knowledge of his child's paternity, or be content in a marriage forced upon him by a king and a conniving wife.

'All yet seems well,' the king says in the play's penultimate line, and this is not an empty turn of phrase, where 'seems' can readily be understood as a synonym for 'is'. The only thing we can be certain about at the end of the play is that we will not get to see whatever problems Bertram and Helena, or Diana and the husband she chooses, will inevitably face in their marriages. A good parallel example can be found at the end of *The Two Gentlemen of Verona*, where Sylvia finally gets to marry her beloved Valentine, and Juliet her beloved Proteus, but only after Proteus has threatened to rape Sylvia and Valentine has offered to 'give' Sylvia to him (5.4.83) as a reward for Proteus repenting the harm he has done to the two men's friendship. Shakespeare's comedies almost always end in or on the point of a marriage, and the last act often works hard to bring about this end – as we see vividly in *Two Gentlemen*, where a band of outlaws (who were, naturally, introduced at the beginning of the fourth act) is instrumental in the multiple undisguisings, reunions and reconciliations with which the play ends. But while a marriage might be an obvious way to end a play, it is just as obviously the beginning of a new and complex social relationship. The action that precedes the last act of a Shakespeare play is (as I have been attempting to demonstrate in the preceding chapters) so complex, multifarious and full, that questions about the future of the characters cannot but press upon us. Dramatic convention alone, that is, the need for closure in a finite, temporal medium, cannot erase the memory of the problems the play has represented, nor extinguish their energy. By introducing new problems – Helena's equivocal triumph, the king's willingness to give Diana the same dubious reward he gave Helena, Proteus's attempted sexual assault – at a moment when there is no time left to address them, Shakespeare pushes against the boundaries of the play itself, refusing to end at the end, asking us to think of all the preceding action as a prologue to a future history we can only imagine.

C.

As exciting as it can be to feel, at the end of a play, that nothing is really finished – that the energy of the preceding action will continue to course through the imaginary future lives of the characters – it can also be frustrating. Frustration is a response Shakespeare seems deliberately to court in his last acts. In *Dream, Titus, All's Well* and *Two Gentlemen*, he does so fairly subtly: you can always second-guess your frustration, and subordinate it to the act's explicit signals of closure. In the plays I discuss in this section, Shakespeare courts frustration, even disappointment, more openly, in large part by refusing to end the play where it seems most likely to end.

Henry V provides a relatively simple example: the play ends with the betrothal of Henry and the princess of France, the naming of Henry as heir to the French throne and the promise of lasting peace between France and England. But the triumphant exit of Henry V and his new French family is followed by the entrance of the chorus, who speaks an epilogue reminding us that Henry V would die young and that the troubled reign of his son, Henry VI, 'in infant bands crowned King' (Epilogue 9), would lead to the loss of French territories and to civil war in England. Moreover, the epilogue reminds us that we had no reason to feel particularly celebratory at the end of the play because the stage 'oft ... hath shown' (13) the tragic unraveling of Henry V's accomplishment – that is, in Shakespeare's own *Henry VI* plays. Ending on this low note might make us notice in retrospect that the triumphant conclusion of the final scene, before the chorus arrives, is riven with tensions: Henry insists on kissing Katherine (5.2.273) in spite of her vehement protests that kissing before marriage is not customary in France (250–65); the French king has attempted to avoid writing into the articles of surrender that Henry will become heir to his throne (329–38); and Katherine does not speak a single word for the last 110 lines of the play. The war has been won, but many battles remain to be fought.

We might say that *Henry V* ends without bringing its action to an end, or we might say that it ends twice: once with a gesture of comic closure and once with a gesture towards tragic history. *Romeo and Juliet* might be said to have three endings. The first comes in the speech the prince speaks after hearing from the friar and Balthasar the events that led to the deaths of Romeo, Juliet and Paris. That speech concludes with these emphatic lines:

> Capulet, Montague,
> See what a scourge is laid upon your hate,
> That heaven finds means to kill your joys with love;
> And I, for winking at your discords too,
> Have lost a brace of kinsmen. All are punished.
>
> (5.3.291–5)

This is bleak, but not inappropriately so; tragedy is supposed to hurt. In its unflinching description of the play's wasteful violence, it resembles the final speeches of *Othello* and *Coriolanus*.

But the play does not end here. Capulet and Montague do not let the prince have the last word.

CAPULET
O brother Montague, give me thy hand.
This is my daughter's jointure, for no more
Can I demand.
MONTAGUE But I can give thee more,
For I will raise her statue in pure gold,
That whiles Verona by that name is known,
There shall no figure at such rate be set
As that of true and faithful Juliet.
CAPULET
As rich shall Romeo's by his lady's lie,
Poor sacrifices of our enmity.

(296–304)

On the face of it, these lines seem to blunt the edge of the prince's: the rival patriarchs agree to end their feud and memorialize their children. Yet even as Capulet and Montague seem committed to moving beyond their ancient rivalry, they create a new one. Capulet rhetorically imagines Montague as impoverished – now that their children are dead, the only 'jointure' (the portion of the husband's property given to his widow) he can settle upon Capulet's daughter is a hand offered in forgiveness – but Montague responds by insisting on his real wealth: he will show just how sorrowful he is for Juliet's death by erecting a statue of her, all in gold. Her worth in posterity (the 'rate' at which her 'figure' will be 'set') will be determined by Montague's ability to commission a rich statue. Capulet, of course, cannot let this pass unmatched: he must pay for a statue of Romeo '[a]s rich' as Juliet's. The resolution of the feud is tinged with the slightest hints that it might flare up again.

Capulet's final lines in the quoted passage create a rhymed couplet, and, considering the action of the play as a whole, a relatively optimistic one: Romeo and Juliet have been made 'sacrifices' to the family feud, but they do at last get to lie side by side, husband and wife even in death. The play could end here, closed, as Shakespeare's plays almost always are, by a couplet. It is equally conventional, however, for Shakespeare's plays to end with a speech by the highest-ranking character onstage, and so Capulet does not get the last word after all. The prince now speaks again: 'A glooming peace this morning with it brings. / The sun for sorrow will not show his head' (305–6). However lustrous the fathers might imagine their children's golden monument, the clouds of sorrow that hang over Verona will not easily be dissipated. Instead of the lovers' eternity of symbolic repose, the prince looks ahead to the more immediate and unpleasant task of earthly judgement: 'Some shall be pardoned and some punished' (308). He concludes with a couplet whose first line expands the perspective offered at the end of his previous speech, insisting upon the enduringly sorrowful rather than redemptive quality of the action: 'For never was a story of more woe'. The second ends on a rhyme that requires the awkward transposition of the names in the title: 'Than this of Juliet and her Romeo'. This sounds, poetically, as strained as the fathers' claim that their children's death will increase their value. Each time it seems to end, and when it finally ends, the play sounds a hollow note.

Conclusion

For at least two reasons, coming to the end of a Shakespeare play is always a little disappointing. First, the plays are vivid, multifarious and written with a profound and detailed understanding of how people talk to and think about one another and themselves; it is disappointing that we can not continue to watch their characters do and say things. Second, there are so many complex conflicts and strands of action to resolve at the end of the play that Shakespeare doesn't even try to resolve them all: rather, he relies heavily on the conventional mechanisms of closure (marriage, obligatory festivity, perfunctory social and political reconciliations, forceful and narrow moral judgements) while allowing most of the urgent questions or problems raised by the play to remain unanswered or unresolved. The plays never end, indeed it is probably not possible for them to end, with the same grandeur and resonance that characterizes their action. Perhaps Shakespeare himself was disappointed to reach the end of any play; in any case he seems to have been acutely aware that the conventional mechanisms of closure were wholly inadequate to the task of giving the play a meaningful shape. The meaningful shape, elusive and constantly shifting, comes into and goes out of view as the reader or spectator moves through the play, scene by scene and act by act.

CHAPTER TEN

Last Words

Overview

The last words a given character speaks, or the last words of a given play, are as important as first words in representing a compact, complex and often contradictory view of the character who speaks them or the action of the play they conclude. In this chapter, building upon the previous chapter's discussion of the forceful but often inadequate or anticlimactic gestures towards closure that occur in Shakespeare's last acts, I discuss different kinds of last words. In section A, I discuss words spoken by characters just before they die. In section B, I discuss characters who disappear unexpectedly from their plays, and whose last words we have no reason to think of *as* their last. In section C, I discuss the words that bring Shakespeare's plays to an end.

A.

'Nothing in his life / Became him like the leaving it,' says Malcolm of the rebellious Thane of Cawdor, who is executed early in the first act of *Macbeth* (1.4.7–8). According to report, Cawdor 'very frankly … confessed his treasons, / Implored your highness' pardon, and set forth / A deep repentance' (5–7). His death is the perfect performance of a noble, courageous traitor. Many of Shakespeare's characters have deaths like this, where their last words are precisely expressive of who they are, or of how they hope to be remembered.

'I kissed thee ere I killed thee,' says Othello to the dead body of Desdemona: 'no way but this, / Killing myself, to die upon a kiss' (5.2.356–7). In the long speech that he makes just before stabbing himself (5.2.336–54), Othello emphasizes his identity as a warrior, but as he dies, he thinks of himself as a lover, and he accepts, with soldier-like courage, that love and violence are inextricably intertwined. We do not have to accept these last words as the most accurate representation of the play's terrible events to see that they correspond to a strong idea Othello has held about himself throughout the play. Coriolanus's last words before he is killed by a rout of Volscians are similarly consistent with both his virtues and his failings throughout the play: 'O that I had him,' he says of Aufidius, who has accused him for a traitor, 'With six Aufidiuses, or more, his tribe, / To use my lawful sword' (5.6.128–9). Here as throughout the play Coriolanus is a solitary figure ready to take on the world: his willingness to stand alone is both his most compelling, indeed most virtuous, quality and his most intractable failing.

Of course, not every character gets the last words that he or she would want, or that we would expect. The always loquacious Hotspur, surprised to find himself slain on the battlefield by Prince Hal, realizes that he is running out of words but tries to the last to keep speaking.

> O, I could prophesy,
> But that the earthy and cold hand of death
> Lies on my tongue. No, Percy, thou art dust,
> And food for –
>
> (5.4.82–5)

We can be sure that it would be very galling for Hotspur, always so heedless of interruptions (see, for example, 1.3.193–255), to know not only that his speech was cut off by death but that his sentence was finished by his rival: 'For worms, brave Percy,' says Hal (86). It is a slightly comic moment that reflects poorly on the prince – ever the tavern-wit, he cannot resist getting the last laugh – and that dramatizes once again the close connection between two men who can only see themselves as opposites.

The final scene of *Othello* makes similarly clever use of a character's dying words to dramatize the dynamic movement between connection and opposition that characterizes Othello and Desdemona's marriage. When Othello smothers Desdemona she is able to say nothing more than 'O Lord! Lord! Lord!' (5.2.83), a horribly realistic prayer for help. But, as it turns out, these are not Desdemona's last words: although Othello believes his wife to be dead (see 5.2.90), when Emilia enters the room with news of the violence outside Bianca's house, Desdemona suddenly revives. 'O falsely, falsely murdered!' she cries at line 115, and 'A guiltless death I die' at 121; these are last words that we might hope and expect to hear from a character whom we have seen to be both extremely self-possessed and entirely innocent throughout the play. Yet Desdemona still has not spoken her last words. 'O, who hath done this deed?' Emilia asks, to which Desdemona replies, 'Nobody. I myself. Farewell. / Commend me to my kind lord – O, farewell!' (121–3). These lines are rather a puzzle. Why would Desdemona, who has just proclaimed herself guiltless, suddenly exculpate her husband and blame herself? Now that she is talking, we probably hope that she will continue to talk – that she will make some sense of her last pronouncement. It is one of the play's cruelest ironies that these really are Desdemona's last words, and that Othello immediately uses them against her, twice: 'You heard her say herself it was not I' (125) and 'She's like a liar gone to burning hell: / 'Twas I that killed her' (127–8).

As with the ends of his scenes, his acts and his plays, Shakespeare liked to create and play upon uncertainty in the last words spoken by dying characters. Here as everywhere in both his plays and his poetry, he was reluctant to foreclose possibilities for multiple meanings and alternative, future actions. Although Roderigo's death at Iago's hand (accompanied by the wonderful last words 'O damned Iago! O inhuman dog!', 5.1.62) is an accepted fact of 5.1 and 5.2, we learn from Cassio, just before Othello's suicide, that 'even but now [Roderigo] spake, / After long seeming dead' (5.2.325–6). Does this mean that Roderigo is now alive, or that he, like Desdemona, revived just long enough to speak before really dying? There is no way to answer this question certainly. In *Antony and Cleopatra* 4.9, the heartbroken Enobarbus is observed by some watchmen and a sentry as he walks late at night, accusing himself of being a traitor to his master. 'O Antony! O Antony!' he cries (26) – fitting, tragic last words, certainly – and the watchmen and sentry run to him. A watchman thinks that 'he sleeps' (30) while the sentry says that he 'Swoons rather' (31). The sentry then revises his opinion – 'The hand of death hath raught him' (36) – and is almost immediately contradicted by another watchman: 'He may recover yet' (40). Enobarbus is carried off the stage and out of the play, never to be mentioned again, suspended between death and life.

B.

While Enobarbus may not return to the play physically, his loyalty to Antony (even in deserting him) and his overwhelming outpouring of grief for what has become of their friendship are meant to stay with us, standing in sharp contrast to Cleopatra's calculating, self-regarding actions leading up to Antony's death and her own. Her last words are an echo of Enobarbus's: 'O Antony' (5.2.311). As in all other areas of Shakespeare's dramatic structure and poetic patterning, when an important gesture or idea is strangely unfulfilled or seems to disappear, it usually gets fulfilled or reappears in a different form elsewhere in the play.

In *As You Like It* 2.6, Orlando and his late father's former servant Adam are lost in the forest; Adam is desperately hungry.

> Dear master,
> I can go no further. O, I die for food!
> Here lie I down and measure out my grave.
> Farewell, kind master.
>
> (2.6.1–4)

These sound as if they could be Adam's last words. But when, in the next scene, Orlando comes upon a forest banquet being held by the exiled Duke and his courtiers, he quickly returns to the shelter where he deposited the old man after the end of the previous scene, and then carries him in to the banquet, where he is given a seat at the table.

> DUKE
> Welcome. Set down your venerable burden
> And let him feed.
> ORLANDO
> I thank you most for him.

ADAM So had you need;
I scarce can speak to thank you for myself.

(2.7.168–71)

Adam presumably spends the remainder of this scene, about thirty lines (including a song), eating, and then exits supported by the duke and Orlando. The Duke says:

Good old man,
Thou art right welcome, as thy master is.
Support him by the arm. Give me your hand
And let me all your fortunes understand.

(201–4)

This sounds like a speech someone might make at the end of a play. And for Adam, it is the end of the play. His last words are those given in the quotation above, and he never appears onstage again. It is easy to imagine that he has died, since he is very old and must continue to live in the woods even after he has been fed; but there is no evidence that he has died, since neither Orlando nor anyone else mentions the fact – or, indeed, mentions Adam at all.

As he does with Desdemona, Shakespeare manipulates our expectations about what might and might not be Adam's last words; as with Enobarbus, he makes sure that Adam is an important part of the play's meaning even after he seems to have been removed from it. Orlando's entrance with Adam in 2.7 is precisely timed to correspond with the last words of Jaques's speech describing the seven ages of man:

Last scene of all,
That ends this strange eventful history,
Is second childishness and mere oblivion,
Sans teeth, *sans* eyes, *sans* taste, *sans* everything.

Enter ORLANDO *bearing* ADAM

(2.7.164–7)

Does Adam in his helplessness, carried by Orlando, embody the truth of Jaques's portrait? Or does he immediately revive upon sitting down to eat, and so reveal Jaques's narrow and cynical perspective? This must remain an open question. In either case, Jaques and Adam represent, together or separately, something about the end of human experience which can be acknowledged but not fully comprehended by the play's overall movement towards renewal and revival. At the end of the final scene we learn that Duke Frederick has in some sense decided to start the play all over again, this time for himself: recognizing his own corruption after a conversation with an 'old religious man' he met 'in the skirts of this wild wood' (5.4.157–8), he has 'thrown into neglect the pompous court' (180) and decided to live in the forest. Jaques plans to join him there and says that he can henceforth be found at Duke Senior's 'abandoned cave' (194). The sudden disappearance of Frederick (his last words occur in 3.1, long before his conversion) and the mention of an old man carry echoes of Adam. Adam's last words, admitting both a dependence upon others and a powerlessness to speak, dramatize a humility that is difficult to find in the characters who remain to celebrate at the end of the play. 'Proceed, proceed!' begin Duke Senior's final lines, as he is apparently in haste to get out of the forest. 'We'll begin these rites / As we do trust they'll end, in true delights' (5.4.195–6). He has nothing to say of his brother's self-imposed exile, and no further entreaties for Jaques to stay.

There are many other examples in Shakespeare's plays of characters whose last words are not the end of the work they do in the play. One is the Duchess of Gloucester in *Richard II*, whose desire to avenge the death of her husband, Thomas of Woodstock, murdered by his own kin, is never again raised so explicitly after her only scene (1.2), but reappears transformed at the end of the play when Bolingbroke says that Exton will suffer the punishment of Cain for helping to murder Richard (5.6.43). Another is the fool in King Lear, who disappears after the third act ('And I'll go to bed at noon' are his last words, at 3.6.82), but who makes a startling return to our consciousness when Lear, holding his dead daughter in his arms, says 'And my poor fool is hanged' (5.3.304. Whether Lear refers here to his fool or to Cordelia is one of the great close-reading puzzles of the Shakespeare canon). A third is Shylock, who departs humbled at the end of 4.1 ('Send the deed after me, / And I will sign it' are his last words at 392–3), and who might be expected to put in an appearance, chastened and converted, in the festive final scene. He does not return to the play, though he does cast a long shadow: he is never mentioned in the romantic banter of Jessica and Lorenzo at the beginning of 5.1; he is referred to only as 'the rich Jew' (5.1.292) when Nerissa tells the lovers that they will inherit Shylock's estate; and as a character who mourned the giving away of a ring given him by his wife (see 3.1.106–11) he stands in implicit contrast to Bassanio and Gratiano who are in the final scene both humiliated and forgiven for a similar crime. That Gratiano, a character said by Antonio in the first act to speak an 'infinite deal of nothing' (1.1.114), is given the play's last word – and, moreover, in the form of an obscene joke (Nerissa's 'ring' is both the love-token she has given her husband and her vagina) – seems like one of the play's cruelest ways of suppressing Shylock, or dramatizing the moral vacuity of the Christians.

One way in which Shakespeare creates the characteristic sense that the action of his plays will continue beyond the end of their performance is to make their last words seem haunted by the presence of characters who surprisingly do not figure in the conclusion.

C.

Conventionally, the last words of plays by Shakespeare and his contemporaries are spoken by the highest-ranking character onstage. Sometimes this can create a climactic effect: the words spoken by Lucius at the end of *Titus Andronicus* (discussed in the previous chapter), however horrifying they might be, are entirely in keeping with the violence of the play, and just what we might expect the future Roman emperor to say of the Gothic queen who unleashed terrible violence upon his family. At the end of *The Winter's Tale*, to take an example from comedy, Leontes leads his newly reunited family offstage so that

> we may leisurely
> Each one demand and answer to his part
> Performed in this wide gap of time since first
> We were dissevered. Hastily lead away.
>
> (5.3.152–5)

In these excited lines there is a sense of both finality and a new beginning. As with Lucius and his family in *Titus Andronicus*, Leontes and his family have been through an extraordinary range of intense and difficult experiences; the last words these characters speak acknowledge that and look ahead excitedly to the challenging work to be done.

But just as often as a play's last words are spoken by someone who has suffered through most of the action, they are spoken by a character who has, until the final scene, been a peripheral figure. In these cases the effect is often anticlimactic. I have already discussed, in the previous chapter, some of the formal qualities that make the final act, and especially the final few speeches, of *Romeo and Juliet* anticlimactic. In the context of this chapter, it can be added that the prince, who speaks the play's last words, appears in only three of the play's scenes: when he arrives at the end of the brawl between the Montagues and Capulets, upbraids them for their constant feuding and orders them to come 'this afternoon / To know our farther pleasure in this case, / To old Freetown, our common judgement place' (1.1.98–100); when he arrives after Mercutio has been killed, banishes Romeo and orders all those present to 'attend our will' – that is, wait upon his judgement (3.1.198); and when he arrives after the lovers are dead, accuses the fathers of killing their children with their feud and promises that, after the recent events have been reviewed, 'Some shall be pardoned and some punished' (5.2.308). The prince is largely disconnected from the events of the play, always arriving on the scene too late, and meting out evidently ineffectual punishments. He has not managed to stop the feuding in all the years it has continued; whatever judgement he passes on the families in old Freetown has no effect on Tybalt, and his banishment of Romeo is an arbitrary gesture at best (as I discuss further below). His having the last word in the play is appropriate only because it is conventional, and that is another reason why his last words feel anticlimactic.

In the prince's final speech we can also find a disparity between what he understands, or hopes to understand, about the action of the play and what other characters, or we ourselves, understand about it. After hearing the friar's lengthy description of the events leading up to the lovers' death, in which perhaps the clearest fact is the friar's own part in facilitating the tragedy, the prince says simply 'We still have known thee for a holy man' (270). He is apparently uninterested in accepting the friar's challenge to decide whether 'aught in this / Miscarried by my fault' (266–7). Then, although neither the friar nor Balthasar nor Paris's page has described anything but the actions of passionate lovers acting impulsively, the prince turns to Montague and Capulet and announces that their children's death is 'a scourge ... laid upon your hate' (292), as though they had ever directly forbade their children's love. (It is worth remembering here that Romeo's first love, Rosaline, was also a Capulet.) There is a carelessness in the prince's attention to the causes of violence which we have seen before: in 3.1 he ignores Benvolio's detailed description of the quarrel between Tybalt, Mercutio and Romeo, and substitutes personal revenge for justice:

> I have an interest in your hates' proceeding.
> My blood for your rude brawls doth lie a-bleeding,
> But I'll amerce you with so strong a fine
> That you shall all repent the loss of mine.
> I will be deaf to pleading and excuses,
> Nor tears, nor prayers shall purchase our abuses,
> Therefore use none. Let Romeo hence in haste,
> Else, when he is found, that hour is his last.
>
> (3.1.190–7)

Not only is the prince ineffectual as a punisher, he also promises punishment where none is warranted. In this respect, 'Some will be pardoned, and some punished' rings hollow. Who is left to be judged at all, other than the friar, whom the prince has just exonerated, or the parents, who are both reconciled and childless? As is often the case with the last words of a Shakespeare play, the prince's last words, read closely, make it sound almost as though he doesn't belong to the play he has been called upon to bring to a close.

The inadequacy of last words, the impossibility of arriving at a comprehensive and objective judgement of the action, is particularly obvious in tragic plays, where the things left to explain and understand are so difficult. Lodovico is an unsatisfying choice for the final speech of *Othello*, even though he is, as the representative of the Venetian government, an entirely appropriate one. Henry Richmond in *Richard III* and Malcolm in *Macbeth* are colourless foils to the title characters they displace. Their final speeches are full of ponderous repetition and administrative business: 'All this divided York and Lancaster,' says Richmond, summing up the recent civil wars, 'Divided in their dire division' (5.5.27–8); 'My thanes and kinsmen, / Henceforth be earls, the first that ever Scotland / In such an honour named' is Malcolm's rousing beginning (5.9.28–30). These speeches are in stark contrast to the kinetic last words of Richard III and Macbeth – 'A horse, a horse, my kingdom for a horse!' (*Richard III* 5.4.7); 'Lay on, Macduff, / And damned be him, that first cries, "Hold, enough!"' (*Macbeth* 5.8.33–4) – and to the silence of each character at the moment of his death (see stage directions for *Richard III* 5.5.0 and for *Macbeth* 5.8.34). In their very insistence on closure, Richmond and Malcolm stamp the life out of their plays.

Conclusion

A reader or spectator closes the book or leaves the theatre with the play's last words ringing in his or her head; often, as I have tried to demonstrate in this chapter, those words make a hollow sound. Even the satisfying last words spoken by important characters prove to be full of tension once you look at them closely. 'The rest is silence,' Hamlet tells Horatio (5.2.342), which is powerful indeed: even Hamlet's overflowing mind must meet its limit. But what of his baffling decision to give his 'dying voice,' and thus the kingdom of Denmark, to Fortinbras, the son of his father's enemy? Surely this decision will provoke something more than silence among the Danes. 'Caesar, now be still,' says Brutus after he has run upon his own sword; 'I killed not thee with half so good a will' (*Julius Caesar* 5.5.51–2). A stoic rebel, Brutus, as he acknowledges the failure of his great enterprise, is more eager for his own death than he ever was for Caesar's. Yet the idea that his death will quell the violent forces the assassination set in motion – 'Caesar, now be still' – is another example of the myopia we see in Brutus throughout the play, as he constantly miscalculates the political consequences of decisions he takes for personal reasons. The last words of any character in a Shakespeare play, whether spoken on the point of death or as the means of bringing the play to an end, are probably not the words he or she would speak if he or she could imagine the continuation of the action which the play makes it possible for the reader or spectator to imagine.

PART THREE

CHAPTER ELEVEN

Patterned Language

Overview

The expository and thematic content of any speech, scene, act or play of Shakespeare is expressed through and by means of overlapping patterns of sound, syntax, words, images and ideas. Patterns of sound and syntax will be discussed in Chapter Thirteen. This chapter will be concerned with patterns of images, words and ideas. In section A, I discuss an elaborate pattern of imagery in *Macbeth* that is comparatively easy to see. In section B, I focus on *All's Well That Ends Well*, and discuss a pattern of words that sometimes obviously and sometimes subtly expresses one of the play's main expository and thematic concerns; my analysis of this pattern follows directly from my discussion of the play's title in Chapter One. In section C, I discuss a pattern of ideas in *Richard II* in which, to define and to analyse it, it is necessary to perceive the interaction of patterns of words and patterns of images.

A.

Macbeth is full of birds. The first two appear in the play's second scene, when the bleeding captain explains that the renewed attack of the Norwegian army no more dismayed Macbeth and Banquo than 'sparrows [dismay] eagles' (1.2.35). The last two appear in 5.3

when Macbeth tears into the frightened servant who brings him news of the approaching English army:

> The devil damn thee black, thou cream-faced loon.
> Where got'st thou that goose look?
>
> (5.3.11–12)

To be sure, *Macbeth* is replete with animal imagery. The captain mentions lions undismayed by hares in the second half of 1.2.35, and at the beginning of 5.7 Macbeth imagines himself as a bear tied to a stake – but birds are named more frequently, and with more intensity and variety than any other. Listening for birds between 1.2 and 5.3, we might come to experience Macbeth's Scotland as a veritable aviary: there is the raven on Lady Macbeth's battlements (1.5.38), the martlets that nest in the buttresses of the Macbeths' castle (1.6.3–10), the owl that shrieks after Duncan's murder (2.2.3), the 'obscure bird' that disturbed Lennox's sleep on the same night (2.3.59), the falcon 'hawked at and killed' by a 'mousing owl' on the Tuesday before the king's murder (2.4.11–13), the crow that signals the onset of night as it 'Makes wing to th' rooky wood' (3.2.52), the 'kites' that Macbeth imagines feasting on dead bodies when he sees the ghost at the banquet (3.4.70), the 'maggot-pies and choughs and rooks' whose terrible auguries he contemplates in the same scene (3.4.123) and the 'vulture' of Malcolm's hypothetical lust (4.3.74). Before they are set upon by Macbeth's hired killers, Lady Macduff talks with her son about his potentially fatherless existence in terms of the lives of birds (4.2.31–7), and when one of the murderers stabs young Macduff, he refers to him derisively as 'you egg' (4.2.85). In the next scene, when Macduff receives news that his wife and children have been slaughtered, he refers to them as his 'pretty chickens' and Macbeth as a 'hellkite' (4.3.219–21). What makes these bird references a significant pattern, over and above their frequency, is the consistency with which they are used. With a single exception, all of the bird allusions listed above occur in, or are used to describe, moments of extreme psychic, physical or emotional distress. And even the one exception, the passage about martlets, has an extremity of its own. Banquo points to the presence of the 'temple haunting martlet' as evidence of the hospitable quality of Macbeth's castle. But it is not just one martlet that he sees as he speaks:

No jutty frieze,
Buttress, nor coin of vantage, but this bird
Hath made his pendent bed and procreant cradle.

(1.6.6–8)

In the castle, as in the play, there are birds everywhere.

To begin to interpret the pattern, it is useful to have some idea in mind of the play's thematic priorities. To me, it seems that Shakespeare was interested in birds primarily because the play is about attempting to see into the future, and many birds – in particular ravens, owls and magpies – have traditional associations with augury. Lady Macbeth, Macbeth and the old man in 2.4 speak of birds as signs of present and future events in the human world; Lennox, kept awake while camping en route to Macbeth's house, could not have guessed what the noisy 'obscure bird' portended, but he clearly had a sense that it portended something; as Banquo enters the castle he reads – perhaps misreads – the presence of birds as a good sign, but a sign nevertheless. In a reading of the play that sees augury and portents as central concerns, the birds in the conversation between Lady Macduff and her son in 4.2, or in Macbeth's screaming at the servant in 5.3, resonate with the general significance of the pattern: although they are not specifically presented as omens, in each case the reference to birds precedes a terrible event that has in some sense been foretold.

Of course it is possible to have a reading of *Macbeth* that puts less emphasis on shadows of the future and more emphasis on the political violence and predation that occurs in the present. In this kind of reading, the bird imagery would have a slightly different significance. Almost all the birds mentioned in the play are birds of prey or carrion birds, and almost all the other kinds of birds are represented as helpless (the sparrow before the eagle, Macduff's chickens before the hellkite Macbeth). All the references to birds occur in the context of recent, imminent or planned violence, even when, as in the 'martlets' speech, the speaker seems unaware of his proximity to it. The references to predatory birds describe Macbeth in two ways: as a violent force whose regicide dangerously inverts political and even natural hierarchies – this is suggested by the image of the mousing owl killing a falcon in 2.4; and as a violent force that mimics the brutality of a nature unbound by human feelings or laws – this is suggested by the Captain's reference to sparrows and eagles and, especially, by Macduff's image of the hellkite and the chickens.

These two readings of the play and of the bird imagery are hardly incompatible, and they coalesce around the passage in 2.4. The old man's description of bird behaviour is intended to be read as a sign of the disposition of human events, and what it reveals is a world of ruthless violence where 'naturally' powerful figures (including the soon-to-be-crowned Macbeth) can never be certain of their place at the top of the food chain. Other readings are certainly possible, but the reading you come up with for the pattern is less important than the technique involved in enumerating and correlating its different parts. *Macbeth* is a good play with which to model the technique, because it is so densely patterned: references to clothing, babies, blood and walking occur with the same range and intensity that we find in the bird imagery. The work of interpreting these images begins simply by reading and rereading the play carefully enough to notice the repetition of similar or closely related images in similar or closely related contexts.

B.

Macbeth is not a play about birds; it is a play about regicide, ambition, futurity and any number of other things, in which references to birds are important not for their expository function so much as for their capacity to point to something beyond themselves. Patterned language in Shakespeare often works this way: the images that make up the pattern do not arise from, but rather supplement, the action, providing opportunities for the reader to reflect on and interpret it.

The pattern I will discuss in *All's Well That Ends Well* works differently: it is a pattern not primarily of images but rather of related words and actions that express some of the play's most obvious expository and thematic concerns. The pattern begins with the word *Well* in the play's title. Before you know what the play is about, this word carries only a very general sense: 'Anything that happens is OK as long as everything works out in the end.' If you are an observant reader, you might realize that the more specific meaning of 'well' – 'in health' – is pertinent to the play's action when, at the beginning of the first scene, you learn that the king is sick: 'He hath abandoned his physicians,' Lafew tells the countess at line 12, and a few lines later he informs the curious Bertram that the source of the illness is a fistula (31). Helena's recently deceased father, we also learn in this scene, was a physician. If only he were living, the countess says, 'it would be the death of the king's disease' (21–2). The other thing we learn in this scene is that Helena is in love with Bertram, but despairs of having her love requited due to their different social positions: ''twere all one / That I should love a bright particular star / And think to wed it, he is so above me' (83–5). That Helena thinks of this love as an illness is clear from the two lines with which she begins her final speech in the scene, where she begins to formulate a plan for acquiring Bertram's love:

> Our remedies oft in ourselves do lie,
> Which we ascribe to heaven ...
>
> (212–13)

A 'remedy', generally, is any means of 'counteracting a source of misery or difficulty' (*OED* 1), and, more specifically, a 'cure for a disease ... a medicine or treatment' (*OED* 2). The plan that Helena hits upon, rather obliquely expressed at this point, has to do with drawing upon the knowledge and skills imparted to her by her physician father: 'Who ever strove / To show her merit that did miss her love?' she asks (222–3), and then announces that her 'project' is focused on the 'king's disease' (226). By the end of the first scene of *All's Well*, two plots are set in motion and intertwined: one has to do with curing the king's physical sickness, the other with curing Helena's love-sickness. The word *sick* occurs five times in the first and second acts, and in four of these (1.2.74, 1.3.131, 2.1.167, 2.3.111), it is connected either to the king's disease or to Helena's love for Bertram.

All's Well, then, is a play explicitly about sickness and health, and you can trace fairly elaborate patterns of language, explicit and implicit, related to these primary concerns. At the beginning of the second scene, the king and his lords discuss the war between Florence and Siena currently underway in Italy, and the desire of young Frenchmen to join the conflict; the king is reluctant to take sides in the conflict, but he is happy for his subjects to 'stand on either part' (1.2.15). 'It well may serve / A nursery to our gentry,' replies of one of his lords, 'who are sick / For breathing and exploit'

(15–17). This is the one use of *sick* in the first two acts that I left out of my list above. What will become the play's third plot, Bertram's flight to Italy and what happens to him there, is introduced here by a medical metaphor. This metaphor will be repeated in 3.1 when the action moves to Italy, and a French lord, speaking to the Duke of Florence of the willingness of young French men to fight in his cause, says that he is 'sure the younger of our nature / That surfeit on their ease will day by day / Come here for physic' (3.1.17–19).

Bertram, of course, comes to Italy not only to find a cure for his indolence but also, and more directly, to get away from Helena; and while he does seem to prove his own valour in the wars (see 3.5.1–9), he also spends much of his time attempting to seduce the Florentine maiden Diana. The word 'sick', which disappears for a time after the king is cured, reappears in the very midst of the Diana plot: 'Stand no more off,' Bertram implores her,

> But give thyself unto my sick desires,
> Who then recovers. Say thou art mine, and ever
> My love as it begins shall so persever.
>
> (4.2.334–7)

These are perhaps the exact words that Helena would most wish to hear from Bertram. The strong sense the play gives us that Bertram behaves badly towards Helena (even though he might be justified in chafing at a marriage forced upon him) comes in part from his making expedient use of a metaphor that is rooted in the action where Helena acts virtuously. And Bertram remains expedient almost to the very end, rejecting Parolles's report against him with these words:

> He's quoted for a most perfidious slave
> With all the spots a' th' world tax'd and debosh'd,
> Whose nature sickens but to speak a truth.
> Am I or that or this for what he'll utter,
> That will speak anything?
>
> (5.3.204–8)

Bertram's humiliation and exposure in the rest of the scene is meant to demonstrate how much he has in common with Parolles. Bertram is the sick one, and accepting Helena as his wife is the first step towards self-healing. Of course, like the king in the first part of the play, he has a choice whether to accept Helena's healing medicine or not: 'All yet seems well,' the king says in the play's final lines, 'and if it end so meet, / The bitter past, more welcome is the sweet' (5.3.327–8). The general and the medical senses of the word 'well' are both present here, but the king's 'seems' and 'if' (as I have discussed in section B of Chapter 9) suggest that the danger of sickness is never entirely past.

The difficult problems the characters must overcome for all to be well are both physical and social. As we know from the first scene, the king has been suffering from a fistula: this is a burrowing, suppurating abscess – an image of lurking corruption. Bertram and Helena, meanwhile, must find a way to transcend deeply entrenched class differences. These problems are described in medical terms, and presented as something the king himself might be able to 'cure' in 2.3, when he insists to Bertram that Helena is virtuous and for that reason worthy of Bertram's love in spite of her low social position.

> Where great additions swell's and virtue none,
> It is a dropsied honour.
>
> (2.3.126–7)

People with great titles but little virtue are merely swollen by those titles, just as a person who suffers from dropsy (now more commonly referred to as oedema) is swollen by excess fluid in the tissues. This diagnostic metaphor is preceded by the king's claim that distinctions in 'blood' have no inherent basis; here again, he looks inside the body.

> Strange is it that our bloods,
> Of colour, weight, and heat, pour'd all together,
> Would quite confound distinction, yet stands off
> In differences so mighty.
>
> (2.3.118–21)

The mingling of bloods the king imagines here – a scientific experiment that clearly demonstrates fundamental likeness – is not something that can happen in the world of the play. Rather, Bertram's and Helena's bloods are mingled by an act of sexual trickery perpetrated under cover of darkness (just as the king's disease must be cured by a secret process), and the proof of its having happened must await the birth of the child Helena claims to be carrying in the play's final scene.

The three strands of action in *All's Well* are causally connected – Helena's love causes her to cure the king's disease, and when the king rewards her Bertram goes to Italy – and are linked thematically by the word 'sick', the idea of 'disease' and images of things that can come out of a body: pus (from the king's abscess), blood (a word that signifies status) and babies (the end of marriage and the beginning of life). The word 'well', occurring twice in the title and dozens of times over the course of the play, is part of this patterning, but usually only implicitly. In only one passage, at the beginning of 2.4, is 'well' used in the sense 'in health': Helena, residing at the French court, has received a letter from the countess by way of her servant Lavatch. 'My mother greets me kindly,' she says; 'is she well?' Lavatch, a satirical clown, replies: 'She is not well, but yet she has her health' (1–2). You can see from this passage that Shakespeare had the play's overall medical idea in mind when he gave it its title; by using 'well' almost exclusively in its general sense, he fills the word with potential energy. It is both closely connected to and in tension with the 'sick' pattern that structures so much of the action. This is one means by which Shakespeare's poetic language is able to imply more than it says: words carry meanings and potential meanings in multiple contexts. These meanings can be overlaid onto the action, as in my examples from *Macbeth*; directly connected to the action, as in my examples from *All's Well*; or both, as in the examples from *Richard II*, which I shall discuss in the next section.

C.

Richard II is a play of tears. The first that we hear of are the Duchess of Gloucester's, as she promises to live out her days mourning her husband's murder (1.2.71–4). At the beginning of 1.4, Richard wonders sardonically whether any tear was shed at the banished Bolingbroke's departure, and is assured by Aumerle that none was (1.4.1–9). After the first act, once John of Gaunt has died and Henry Bolingbroke has returned to press his claim for inheritance – and then the throne – tears are mostly associated with King Richard and his separation from kingdom, queen or both (see, among others, 2.2.14–27, 3.1.14–16, 3.2.4–11, 3.3.155–69, 3.3.202–3, 3.4.19–23, 4.1.184–9, 4.1.327–34, 5.1.8–10, 5.2.27–36 and 5.4.51–4), but we also find them in the subplot involving Aumerle's treason (see 5.3.100–3) and in Bolingbroke's final words as he looks upon the coffin of Richard II (5.6.49–52). In all these instances, tears are the sign of a deeply felt loss. In the most important thematic sense, tears might be said to represent the condition of kingship: in an elaborate metaphor of two buckets in a well in 4.1, Richard identifies himself as the bucket 'down and full of tears' (4.1.188) and in the final speech of the play Bolingbroke declares that his soul is 'full of woe' over the death of Richard (5.6.45).

The pattern of tears in *Richard II* has an expository basis: that is, all the characters have good reason to cry. But the tears in the play are also part of a larger pattern of water imagery that is overlaid onto the action, primarily for metaphorical purposes and often in conjunction with imagery of fire. In the play's opening lines, Richard calls in the judicial combatants Bolingbroke and Mowbray, saying that they are both 'full of ire, / In rage, deaf as the sea, hasty as fire' (1.1.18–19). This is the first of several images in the play that represent political conflicts and the forces that underlie them as elemental: see also Gaunt's description of Richard's personality at 2.1.33–6; Richard's description of the power of kingship at 3.2.36–62 (where the fiery eye of heaven seeks out traitors on behalf of a king whose anointing balm cannot be washed off by 'all the water in the rough rude sea'); and Bolingbroke's imagining of the meeting between himself and Richard at 3.3.54–60. Also connected to this pattern are Gaunt's description of England as (among other things) a nation protected by 'the triumphant sea' (2.1.61–4); the gardener's promise to plant 'a bank of rue' in a place where the queen let fall a tear (3.4.102–7); Richard's claim that 'water cannot wash away' the sin Northumberland has committed in assisting Bolingbroke's rebellion (4.1.242); and Bolingbroke's imagining his kingship as a flower growing from the blood 'sprinkle[d]' by Richard's murder (5.6.45–6). When characters cry in *Richard II*, their tears fall into a pattern of liquid imagery that surrounds and flows through most of the speaking and thinking about political and personal conflict and loss in the play.

Late in 4.1, after Richard has been presented with the articles of deposition, the king laments his helplessness with a wish that he had always been as inconsequential as he has now been made to be:

> Alack the heavy day,
> That I have worn so many winters out
> And know not now what name to call myself.
> O, that I were a mockery king of snow,
> Standing before the sun of Bolingbroke,
> To melt myself away in water-drops!
>
> (4.1.257–62)

Trying to give shape to the emptiness he feels, Richard draws together the language of cold and heat, of water, and of tears into a single striking image: the melting snowman. The image seems to be suggested to Richard by the line about wearing 'many winters out'; once it has been created, the image calls forth its opposite, the sun, but even in this moment of loss Richard retains, through poetry, some power for himself: although he stands before the sun of Bolingbroke, he melts *himself* away. The sorrow he feels is his alone. As we see in the lines that follow the snow-king passage, where he examines his face in a mirror that he then smashes on the floor, Richard enjoys imagining his identity dispersed into many minute parts – 'water-drops', 'an hundred shivers' (289) – that retain his sorrowful essence and elude Bolingbroke's grasp.

Conclusion

To begin analysing Shakespeare's patterned language, it is necessary simply to look for words and images that repeat. The effect of any pattern lies not only in the repetition of, but also the variation between, like or related elements. In a work of dramatic poetry, variations in words (e.g. all the different birds in *Macbeth*), context (e.g. the word 'sick' occurring in the different plots of *All's Well*) and image (e.g. 'sea', 'tears', 'king of snow' and 'sprinkle' in *Richard II*) are invitations to interpretation. The work of interpretation involves tracing the pattern in as much detail as possible, and trying to articulate a relation between any one element and any other, and between any one or more elements and the larger expository and thematic concerns of the play. As I have tried to demonstrate, articulating a relation between the elements in a pattern is in fact a powerful way of reaching a detailed understanding of a play's larger expository and thematic concerns.

I have focused in this chapter on patterns that extend throughout the plays in which they occur and that express their plays' central concerns. But patterns need not be extensive or thematically significant to be worth noticing as instances of Shakespeare's complex poetic language. Henry IV's first speech in *1 Henry IV* contains a minor pattern of words pertaining to feet: the 'armed hoofs' that have bruised the landscape in the recent civil war (1.1.8); the formerly opposed soldiers who now 'March all one way' rather than in opposition (15); and the 'blessed feet' of Christ, which Henry imagines walking on the holy land where crusading English soldiers will soon 'chase' pagans (24–5). When, at the end of the speech, Henry says that it is 'bootless' to inform everyone once again of his desire to undertake a crusade, he means that it is 'to no purpose' (*OED* 3), but the word resonates discreetly with the other foot-related words in the passage. That Shakespeare and his audiences readily heard the sound of 'boot' meaning 'covering for the foot that extends above the ankle' (*OED* n.3, 1a) in the word 'boot' meaning 'Good advantage, profit, use' (*OED* n.1, 1a) is clear from 3.1.66–8 of this play, where Hotspur puns sardonically on the two words. One would be hard-pressed to develop a boot-centred interpretation of *1 Henry IV*, but the word does participate in a local pattern that is part of the poetic complexity and coherence of the opening speech. Similarly, *Romeo and Juliet* contains multiple references to fish (see 1.1.27–31, 1.2.37–43, 1.3.90–1, 2.4.37–9, 5.1.42–4) which can be said to amount to a pattern, even though it is a pattern that does not seem significant. Especially because the fish words are clustered together in the first part of the play, it is possible to see them as an idea that gets caught in Shakespeare's poetic ear, and which he elaborates for its own sake while he is developing much more explicit, thematically important patterns of language and imagery (stars, light and dark, flowers and herbs, books, etc.). All patterns are not equally significant, but the density, complexity and interest of Shakespeare's poetic language reside in his development of patterns of all kinds.

CHAPTER TWELVE

Characters

Overview

On the page and in the theatre, the poetic language of Shakespeare's plays is embodied in dramatic characters: imaginary persons intended to be brought to life by actors, or in the mind of the reader. Describing and interpreting the relationships and personalities of dramatic characters is the primary activity of most readers and spectators of Shakespeare's plays; as is probably evident from the foregoing chapters, a great deal of the close reading done by teachers and scholars of Shakespeare's plays is in support of this activity. In this chapter I demonstrate some ways of analysing characters as elements of dramatic form. My focus here is not primarily on questions of personality and motivation, for I think a good actor or an imaginative reader can imbue a given character with a very wide range of personalities, and their actions with an equally wide range of motivations: a relaxed and good-humoured Iago or a resentful and frenetic Iago are equally possible, as are an Iago who seems to be driven by revenge for being passed over for promotion by Othello and an Iago whose malignity seems essentially motiveless. Rather than personality and motivation, my focus is primarily on action – on how the action affects what a character might be from one scene to the next, and on how a spectator's or a reader's shifting view of a character affects his or her view of the action. As with everything else I have discussed in this book, any single Shakespearean character usually is and does more than one thing at a time.

In section A of this chapter I focus on Hamlet, the archetypal Shakespearean character, and offer some ways of analysing the relation between character and action through the soliloquy. In section B, I track an important but peripheral character, Paris in *Romeo and Juliet*, through that play to show how a character can embody or enable multiple perspectives on the action. In section C, I focus on a minor, nameless character, the courtesan in *The Comedy of Errors*, to show how detailed and subtle Shakespeare is in working out, through the relationships between characters, the expository and thematic implications of a play's action.

A.

The most obvious place to see what a character is and does is the soliloquy: a speech that a character speaks, as it were, to him or herself, usually but not always while alone onstage. Hamlet's first soliloquy occurs in his first scene, and it is only the fifth time he speaks (1.2.129–59). A few lines before this soliloquy, he insists to his mother that, however much the 'forms, moods, [and] shapes of grief' that all can observe in him might seem to be merely 'actions that a man might play', they nevertheless represent the intensity of his grief for his father's death: 'that within which passes show' (82–5). King Claudius takes Hamlet at his word and responds with a lengthy speech about the inevitability of death and of sons losing their fathers, at the end of which he promises to show 'no less nobility of love' towards Hamlet 'Than that which dearest father bears his son' (110–11); the stepfather wishes to become the father. Claudius might leave the stage confident that he has done what is possible by way of comforting his new stepson, but when Hamlet speaks alone, he reveals that there is more to his 'woe' than meets the eye.

> That it should come to this!
> But two months dead – nay, not so much, not two –
> So excellent a king, that was to this
> Hyperion to a satyr, so loving to my mother
> That he might not beteem the winds of heaven
> Visit her face too roughly. Heaven and earth,

Must I remember? Why she would hang on him
As if increase of appetite had grown
By what it fed on. And yet within a month
(Let me not think on't – Frailty, thy name is Woman),
A little month, or e'er those shoes were old
With which she followed my poor father's body,
Like Niobe, all tears. Why, she –
O God, a beast that wants discourse of reason
Would have mourn'd longer – married with my uncle ...

(137–51)

Comparing his uncle to a satyr (a mythical creature traditionally considered lustful), imagining his mother's 'appetite' for his father and comparing her to a 'beast' in her desire to remarry, Hamlet makes clear in this speech that Claudius's attempts to comfort him took exactly the wrong approach. Hamlet is not only, perhaps not even primarily, upset about his father's death, but also, and perhaps even more, about his mother's marriage to Claudius. The method of the scene is to reveal different, and deeper, levels of Hamlet's character gradually: how he seems to others; what he says to others about the relation between how he seems and how he feels; what he says about how he feels when he is alone. Along the way, the scene also gives us at least two perspectives from which to see Claudius: his own (perhaps earnest, perhaps self-deceiving, perhaps both), where he is the stepfather who must take on his new role with conviction, however awkwardly; and Hamlet's (perhaps accurate, perhaps prurient and overly suspicious, perhaps both), where he is a usurper in more ways than one.

In the theatre it is difficult to tell who characters are until they say who they are. This is as true for simple things like name and social status as it is for more complex things like personality and motivation. Thus the playwright must always build a sense of character relationally. So the effect of Hamlet's first soliloquy depends on its relation to his first speech and is best understood as an expression of what he does not say to Gertrude and to Claudius. His second soliloquy (1.5.92–112) is in direct response to the ghost's story of the old king's murder, his third (2.2.484–540) to the player king's performance, his fourth to the opportunity to murder Claudius (3.3.73–96) and his last (4.4.31–65) to the news of Fortinbras's military adventure. In all of these, as well as in the soliloquy he speaks at the end of 3.2 (as he is on his way to see his mother), Hamlet meditates on his own character, either comparing himself to someone else whose decisive actions are not motivated by a passion such as his (2.2, 4.4) or insisting that he has the qualities necessary to do what the ghost has enjoined him to do (1.5, 3.2, 3.3). Even Hamlet's most famous soliloquy, 'To be or not to be' (3.1.55–89), which seems to be a spontaneous articulation of thought, is framed by the presence and potential responsiveness of other characters: Polonius and Claudius have set Ophelia, reading a book, to encounter Hamlet, whom they know is approaching, and they then retire out of sight to eavesdrop (see 42–54). There is no indication in the play-text that Hamlet is aware of the presence of Claudius, Polonius or even Ophelia as he speaks this speech. But the soliloquy is positioned to invite interpretation in terms of how it might sound to its potential listeners. Who Hamlet is to us must be partly defined by what we imagine others might think him to be.

Of course, even when there are no other characters on the stage, a soliloquizing character is never really alone: in a theatre there is always an audience. 'Now I am alone,' Hamlet announces at 2.2.484. It is possible that an actor might speak this line entirely 'to himself', but the whole speech is replete with rhetorical gestures – questions, exclamations, anecdotes, self-accusations and sudden pronouncements – that demand a direct engagement with the spectators. 'Am I a coward?' he asks, peering into the audience; 'Who calls me villain, breaks my pate across' (506–7) – now he virtually dares us to challenge him. Not all soliloquies in Shakespeare are as outwardly directed as Hamlet's third, but this one nicely represents the performative energy that animates all of them. Even an actor playing Hamlet who is so disciplined as to speak every line in this soliloquy 'to himself' must speak it as though he imagines *someone* – some version of himself – listening, on the verge of objecting, interjecting, contradicting: the Shakespearean soliloquy is an effective device for characterization because it allows the actor to show the character in the process of deciding what kind of character he or she is, and involving the audience in that process.

B.

The first speech in *Macbeth* 1.7 is Macbeth's second soliloquy, in which he tries to decide whether he is the kind of character who fears and could endure the earthly and perhaps eternal consequences of regicide:

> If it were done, when 'tis done, then 'twere well
> It were done quickly. If th'assassination
> Could trammel up the consequence, and catch
> With his surcease success: that but this blow
> Might be the be-all and the end-all, here,
> But here, upon this bank and shoal of time,
> We'd jump the life to come.
>
> (1.7.1–7)

But this soliloquy is not the first thing that happens in the scene. The first thing that happens in the scene is action without speech, described in this stage direction:

> *Hautboys. Torches. Enter a Sewer and divers Servants with dishes and service over the stage. Then enter* MACBETH.

The music ('Hautboys' are oboes), lights and servants (a 'Sewer' is the chief servant of the dining room) signal the beginning of the banquet Macbeth has provided to welcome the doomed King Duncan to his castle. The scene juxtaposes Macbeth's murderous musings on an action not yet taken with the present actions of hospitality. It requires a fair amount of logistical effort to dramatize this juxtaposition: oboists must be hired, given a piece of music and cued; supernumeraries must be assigned to carry the torches and the torches must be lit; the servants and sewer must be costumed appropriately and laden with dishes – all for a brief passage over the stage. As we have seen with the examples from *Hamlet*, the full effect of Macbeth's solitary speaking depends upon its relation to something else, here the entrance and exit of mute functionaries who are precisely his opposite.

The importance of the dinner service as a concrete embodiment of the 'double trust' (12) that Macbeth is on the verge of violating becomes still clearer at the end of the soliloquy, when Lady Macbeth interrupts her husband's musings. 'He has almost supped,' she tells him, referring to the king, and then asks, 'Why have you left the chamber?' (29). Macbeth asks: 'Hath he asked for me?' To which his wife replies, with something like surprise: 'Know you not he has?' (30–1). Through this short exchange we can see that Macbeth has not paused, just before dinner, to speak his soliloquy, but rather has left the dinner table, and has been missed. (There is a telling parallel here to 1.3.129–44, Macbeth's first soliloquy, where he stands aside from Banquo, Ross and Angus, 'rapt' (145), while his friends wonder what is on his mind.) The juxtaposition of the orderly, ceremonial dinner service with Macbeth's passionate ruminations might seem to confirm Lady Macbeth's worst fears: the would-be future king of Scotland, facing the terrible act that will give him the crown, cannot help but nervously draw attention to himself, inexplicably leaving the table while hosting the most important of guests. The beginning of 1.7 gives us, through Macbeth's soliloquy, a portrait of a man confronting with eloquent terror his darkest desires, the violence necessary to realize them, and the possibility that they might destroy him. But it also suggests that we might see a man surprisingly unaware of the practical realities of the present moment, perhaps even an incompetent blunderer. All three perspectives work to define Macbeth's character in the ensuing action: as he cruelly pursues Banquo, Fleance and Macduff's family; as he stumbles disastrously through his coronation banquet; and as he is alternately too credulous and too heedless of the witches' prophesies.

I have argued throughout this book, and especially in Part Two, that Shakespeare tends to structure the action of a play in such a way that it gestures towards any number of other possible plays it might have become. He does this with characters as well. In *Macbeth*, different versions of Macbeth's character allow us to glimpse the different kinds of play *Macbeth* might be, or avoids being, on its way to becoming an essentially political tragedy: it might have been the tragedy of a man who cannot make up his mind to act; a domestic tragedy; a bloody farce. As my next example will demonstrate, in order to embody or provide diverse perspectives on the action, a character need not be as central as Macbeth. It is easy to think of Paris in *Romeo and Juliet* as Romeo's rival for Juliet: in his first scene he is introduced as Capulet's favourite and in his final scene he dies by Romeo's hand while coming to mourn at Juliet's tomb. But if you look closely at Paris's part in the play, you can see that he never really gets to play the role of rival – not least because neither he nor Romeo is aware of the other's love for Juliet at any moment in the play.

In 1.2 Paris has come to ask Capulet's blessing in his suit to Juliet, and Capulet is receptive: 'woo her, gentle Paris, get her heart. / My will to her consent is but a part' (15–16). At this point we have not even heard that Romeo loves Juliet (he is still in love with Rosaline) but we know, from the play's title and its prologue, that he will, and we can easily imagine the action unfolding in such a way as to show Juliet entertaining competing suits from him and Paris. In the next scene, we see Lady Capulet trying to persuade Juliet to love Paris, and Juliet's reply, while equivocal, is basically similar to her father's in its emphasis on both personal desire and parental consent.

> I'll look to like, if looking liking move,
> But no more deep will I endart mine eye
> Than your consent gives strength to make it fly.
>
> (1.3.98–100)

In the first act, we know very little about Paris, only that he is attractive (the nurse refers to him as a 'man of wax', that is, well-formed, at 1.3.77), and that he is impatient to marry Juliet ('Younger than she are happy mothers made,' he tells Capulet at 1.2.12). Shakespeare then all but removes him from the play for nearly two acts: he is mentioned by the nurse at 2.4.195–9, but does not appear again until 3.4, after the death of Tybalt, when Capulet decides to marry him to Juliet post-haste. Our lack of knowledge about Paris's character becomes, at this point, a real problem: we know that Juliet cannot prefer him to Romeo, so we must feel some antipathy towards him, but he has also not had an opportunity (he speaks only three-and-a-half lines in 3.4) to prove himself a more or less sympathetic wooer.

Our view of Paris will become more specific when he next appears, at the friar's cell, in 4.1. Here, as he toes Capulet's paternalistic line – 'Immoderately she weeps for Tybalt's death' (6) – our worst suspicions about Paris, and our feeling that he is essentially different from Romeo, may seem to be confirmed: he is not concerned to have Juliet's love reciprocated; he feels entitled to treat her as a wife because her father has approved the match. But, as the friar's aside at lines 16–17 should remind us, this view of Paris is not entirely fair: like Capulet himself, Paris has no idea about Juliet's love for Romeo – and, indeed, the friar makes sure that he continues to have no idea throughout this scene. Depending on the actor, Paris might obtusely interpret Juliet's ironic replies to his affectionate sallies (18–44) as playful, flirtatious equivocations; or he might show some disturbed awareness that Juliet's heart is not in the match. In either case neither Juliet nor the friar gives him any reason not to assume that he will be married on Thursday, and it is this blind certainty, perhaps a naïve hoping-for-the-best, that makes his final two appearances at once comic and pathetic.

In 4.5, Paris is led into the 'dead' Juliet's chamber by the all-too-knowing friar, who cannot resist virtually having a joke at Paris's (and the Capulets') expense: 'Come, is the bride ready to go to church?' (33). The mourning speeches in this scene are written and organized in a very artificial manner so that they cannot avoid sounding hollow: we know that there is no reason for sorrow at this point because Juliet is not really dead, and the speeches of Paris, who has had no time onstage or off to get to know Juliet (much less woo her) must sound the most hollow of all. In the play's final scene Paris arrives at Juliet's tomb, a faithful lover who plans 'Nightly' to 'strew' Juliet's grave with flowers and 'weep' as he does so (17). He assumes – not unreasonably – that Romeo is in the graveyard to deface the monuments of his hereditary enemies (49–57). In the ensuing fight, Romeo kills Paris without knowing who he is and reacts uncomprehendingly to Paris's final line: 'Open the tomb, lay me with Juliet' (73). Even after Romeo sees that it is Paris he has killed, he does not recognize him as a rival for Juliet:

> What said my man when my betossed soul
> Did not attend him as we rode? I think
> He told me Paris should have married Juliet.
> Said he not so? Or did I dream it so?
> Or am I mad, hearing him talk of Juliet,
> To think it was so?
>
> (76–81)

Shrugging off any thought of rivalry, Romeo decides that Paris is 'writ with me in sour misfortune's book', and hastens to bury him 'in a triumphant grave' (82–3). Even in the long speech with which he summarizes much of the play's action, the friar refers to Romeo and Paris more as partners than rivals: in the tomb, he says, he found 'The noble Paris and true Romeo dead' (259).

Generically and structurally, the play makes it very hard to see things from Paris's point of view – that he has good reason to be sure of Juliet's hand, and that he dies in the belief that he is defending her honour against a vengeful Romeo. Conversely, the play is so good at showing us things from Juliet's, and the friar's, point of view that it is easy to feel as though Paris has deliberately tried to interpose himself between Juliet and her true love, and that his death at Romeo's hands is the inevitable end of a lovers' quarrel. Ultimately, Paris's death is an entirely avoidable accident, and in this above all he and Romeo are alike. So great are the social and self-created obstacles to Romeo and Juliet's marriage that Paris is hardly necessary to the action; thematically, however, he is a powerful figure for the blind desire that governs that action.

C.

In the broadest terms, *The Comedy of Errors* is about Egeon and his family: their separation decades ago, described at length in the first act, is balanced by their reunion in the fifth. But the bulk of the play's action is about something else: the troubled marriage of Antipholus of Ephesus and Adriana. When Adriana accosts Antipholus of Syracuse, mistaking him for her husband, she is not merely puzzled that he does not seem to recognize her, but takes his strange attitude as a symptom of a larger problem:

> Ay, ay, Antipholus, look strange and frown;
> Some other mistress hath thy sweet aspects;
> I am not Adriana, nor thy wife.
> The time was once when thou unurged wouldst vow
> That never words were music to thine ear,
> That never object pleasing in thine eye,
> That never touch well welcome to thy hand,
> That never meat sweet-savoured in thy taste,

Unless I spake, or looked, or touched, or carved to thee.
How comes it now, my husband, O, how comes it,
That thou art then estranged from thyself?
'Thyself' I call it, being strange to me
That undividable, incorporate,
Am better than thy dear self's better part.

(2.2.116–29)

I quote this passage at length to show, first, that Shakespeare is at pains to give a sense of the history of Adriana and Antipholus's marriage, if only in general poetic (rather than detailed expository) terms; and, second, that as her language intensifies Adriana begins to talk about marriage in terms that overlap with some of the play's language about twins (see, for example, 1.2.32–8). In this way the error-filled action involving Antipholus of Ephesus and his wife is made parallel to that involving the twins and their parents; both are resolved in the final scene, both somewhat uncertainly, and the former a little more uncertainly than the latter.

At the centre of the story of Adriana and Antipholus of Ephesus's marriage is a character whom the stage directions and speech-headings call 'Courtesan', though her centrality does not become obvious until the fourth act. Antipholus refers to her as 'a wench of excellent discourse' (3.1.109) and the 'hostess' of the Porpentine tavern (119) when he decides to give up the attempt to force his way into his own home. In this scene Antipholus both acknowledges that he has a history with this woman and insists that it is innocent: 'This woman that I mean / My wife – but, I protest, without desert – / Hath oftentimes upbraided me withal' (111–13). He does, nevertheless, make good on his angry decision to 'bestow' (117) upon her the chain that he has ordered for his wife: when the courtesan first appears, at 4.3.46, she mistakenly demands from Antipholus of Syracuse 'the chain you promised me today' (48). She also reveals in this scene that the chain was not merely a gift, but one half of a jewellery-exchange: 'Give me the ring of mine you had at dinner, / Or for my diamond the chain you promised' (70–1). Over the course of the next few scenes, it will be at her instigation that Antipholus of Ephesus is set upon by Dr Pinch and, briefly, bound and imprisoned in a 'dark and dankish vault' (see 5.1.246–54): the courtesan assumes, from Antipholus of Syracuse's baffled response to her request for the chain, that the man she dined with earlier that day must be 'mad' (4.3.82). Just as the staged dinner-service is not strictly necessary to convey the importance of hospitality in *Macbeth*, so the courtesan is not strictly necessary to the near-undoing of Antipholus of Ephesus: his refusal to pay for a chain that the goldsmith insists he has received (see 4.1) is enough to land him in prison. But the courtesan's presence in the play allows Shakespeare to stage a series of moments where the potential for the destruction of Antipholus of Ephesus and Adriana's marriage is real and threatens to take over the action.

In the course of his day, Antipholus of Ephesus endures a series of nightmare scenarios, the improbable realization of all the anxieties that might secretly haunt a successful man: he is locked out of his own house; his good credit is thrown into question; he is supplanted in both house and credit by his younger brother (the fact that Antipholus of Ephesus is the elder twin is carefully established in 1.1); and, most importantly for our purposes here, his wife and his mistress not only meet but seem to collaborate on his punishment. The courtesan decides to seek out Adriana at the end of 4.3, after she decides that Antipholus is mad. She is too crafty to tell Adriana what happened at the tavern earlier that day; rather, because she assumes that his wife is aware of his erratic behaviour, she tells her that 'being lunatic, / He rush'd into my house and took perforce / My ring away' (4.3.94–6). Antipholus cannot, of course, know what has passed between the women, and he almost certainly fears the worst when he sees them approach, accompanied by Dr Pinch, early in 4.4: 'Mark how he trembles in his ecstasy,' the courtesan says at line 52. Strategically, perhaps, Antipholus seems to take no notice of the courtesan in this scene, focusing instead on Pinch and Adriana and attempting to deflect any potential accusations back against his wife: 'Did this companion with the saffron face / Revel and feast it at my house today?' he asks (62–3), referring to Pinch, and throughout the scene he refers to his wife as 'minion' (61), 'harlot' (102) and 'strumpet' (125).

Antipholus is borne away before Adriana has the opportunity to question him about his dalliances with the actual 'strumpet' on the stage, but the mystery of his arrest, when looked into by Adriana, brings these dalliances once more into view. The officer tells Adriana that her husband has been arrested at Angelo's suit, for a sum due 'for a chain your husband had of him' (136). 'He did bespeak a chain for me but had it not,' Adriana replies, with perhaps just the hint of a question, or a brief suspicious glance, directed towards the courtesan. Again the courtesan acts shrewdly.

> When as your husband all in rage today
> Came to my house and took away my ring –
> The ring I saw upon his finger now –
> Straight after did I meet him with a chain.
>
> (138–41)

This is technically true, though it was, of course, Antipholus of Syracuse whom the courtesan met with the chain. But the courtesan wisely does not mention that the chain was promised to her. She has surmised that the chain was meant for Adriana ('It may be so, but I did never see it' is Adriana's circumspect reply (142) to the courtesan's story about seeing the chain) and has calculated that she will be more likely to get her ring back if she is not perceived as a rival.

At the same time, if she is to get her ring back the courtesan must, at this point, go through Adriana, so she sticks close to her across the act-break: when Adriana enters in 5.1, she is still accompanied by both Luciana and the courtesan. The courtesan is a silent, significant presence onstage as Adriana tells the Abbess how she has recently suspected her husband with another woman (5.1.55–67), and as she gives the duke a rather embellished version of the courtesan's description of Antipholus's behaviour:

> ... this ill day,
> A most outrageous fit of madness took him,
> That desp'rately he hurried through the street,
> With him his bondman, all as mad as he,
> Doing displeasure to the citizens
> By rushing in their houses, bearing thence
> Rings, jewels, any thing his rage did like.
>
> (138–44)

Perhaps Adriana here repeats the courtesan's own embellishment of her story, offered up as conversation during the time, between 4.4 and 5.1, when Adriana was seeking her apparently mad, apparently escaped husband. Alternatively, perhaps the embellishments are Adriana's, as she tries to convince herself as well as the duke and the other Ephesians gathered around in the final scene that her husband's interest in jewellery was indiscriminate – not tied to any one person. In either case, the point is that, for Adriana, the only *possible* explanation for the ring her husband is wearing, for the wayward chain, and indeed for the very presence of the courtesan is Antipholus's madness. This gives a great deal of power to the courtesan, who, as always, uses it wisely: when, at line 276, Dromio of Ephesus points to the courtesan and tells the duke that his master 'din'd with her there, at the Porpentine' that afternoon, the courtesan quickly reiterates her earlier story: 'He did, and from my finger snatched that ring' (277). It is only the courtesan's self-interest, her practical sense that 'forty ducats is too much to lose' (4.3.97), that spares Adriana the humiliation of accusing her husband of being an adulterer.

Thus the entrance of Antipholus of Syracuse at line 341, and the alternative explanation it provides for the day's confusions, cannot be the relief for Adriana that it is for her husband. That is probably why she is as laconic, possibly as watchful, as the courtesan through the remainder of the scene. The courtesan presses her advantage with a single line, extremely well-timed to follow the climactic moment of reconciliation, when the duke pardons Egeon.

DUKE
It shall not need: thy father hath his life.
COURTESAN
Sir, I must have that diamond from you.
ANTIPHOLUS OF EPHESUS
There, take it, and much thanks for my good cheer.
(5.1.390–2)

These are magnificently equivocal lines, acknowledging everything, admitting nothing, certainly not ruling out the possibility of future meetings. There is much more understanding dramatized in this moment between Antipholus of Ephesus and the courtesan than there is in the entire scene between Antipholus of Ephesus and either his wife or his long-lost twin brother, neither of whom he ever speaks to directly. It is possible, at the same time, to read in the tense, careful silence between them, a great deal of understanding between Adriana and the courtesan, conventional but unexpected rivals for Antipholus's love. To a large extent the courtesan is irrelevant and unnecessary to the play's complications, but her presence provides one way of dramatizing how much remains to be lost even in their resolution.

Conclusion

In the middle of the second act of *Troilus and Cressida*, the Trojans have a lengthy argument about whether they should return Helen to the Greeks and thus put an end to years of past and future bloodshed. Hector, who is initially in favour of this idea, brings the argument to a conclusion in this way:

> If Helen then be wife to Sparta's king,
> As it is known she is, these moral laws
> Of nature and of nations speak aloud
> To have her back returned. Thus to persist
> In doing wrong extenuates not wrong,
> But makes it much more heavy. Hector's opinion
> Is this in way of truth; yet, ne'ertheless,
> My sprightly brethren, I propend to you
> In resolution to keep Helen still;
> For 'tis a cause that hath no mean dependence
> Upon our joint and several dignities.
>
> (2.2.183–93)

This passage is remarkable for giving us two contradictory versions of Hector's character. In the first five lines, he speaks the 'truth' that everyone knows: Helen was kidnapped; by the lights of both natural and civil laws her kidnapping was wrong; and the continued slaughter of thousands of soldiers and civilians in the name of this wrong only makes it worse. This lucid view of the situation is all the more convincing because Hector prefaces it by chastising his brothers Paris and Troilus for having considered the question 'but superficially' (165), allowing 'the hot passion of distempered blood' (169), rather than cool and objective reasoning, to determine the difference between right and wrong. Having easily contradicted his friends, Hector then goes on to contradict himself with the verbal equivalent of a helpless shrug: 'yet, ne'ertheless'. Keeping Helen is necessary, he says, to maintain the 'dignities' of the Trojans who have fought for her. This sharp turn in the argument is all the more astonishing because it is a restatement of something Paris has just said: 'What treason were it to the ransacked queen, / Disgrace to your great worths, and shame to me, / Now to deliver her possession up / On terms of base compulsion!' (150–3). Instead of remaining, like the reader or spectator, at an objective distance from the false heroism the play relentlessly satirizes, Hector turns out to be inescapably defined by it.

Hector in this scene is a clear instance of the argument I have been making throughout this chapter: Shakespearean characters tend to inhabit often contradictory roles, and those roles give shape to and are shaped by perspectives on the action that are often contradictory too. A good actor playing Hector might easily use the two contradictory parts of this speech to imagine and perform a larger whole: Hector is the kind of tragic character who sees clearly what it is right to do, but cannot do it. Just as easily, a good actor might speak right through the contradiction and so demonstrate that Hector is as self-deluded as the other characters in the play, truly believing that the 'joint and several dignities' of the Trojans are commensurate with 'moral laws / Of nature and of nations', and must be similarly protected. A third alternative might be that Hector, warming to his own convictions ('Hector's opinion / Is this in way of truth'), suddenly realizes that he is in dangerous territory, on the verge of being ostracized or reprimanded; his self-contradiction in the second half of the speech might then be the result of wary calculation, and the force of truth in the first half not dissipated but held in suspension. Each different version of Hector might entail a different version of the other characters in the scene, of the scene itself, of its relation to the scenes around it, and of the relation of all of these to the entire play – whose climactic tragic scene does not involve the title characters but rather the unarmed Hector futilely imploring the armed Achilles to '[f]orgo' his 'vantage' (5.9.9). Working out who a character is and what he or she does is probably the most productive and imaginatively rewarding way to begin reading a play closely – not least because it requires you to draw upon all the other close reading methods described in this book.

PART FOUR

CHAPTER THIRTEEN

Metre

Overview

The language of Shakespeare's plays and poems is, for the most part, metrical language. It is written according to formal conventions that depend on more or less precise units of measurement: the line, usually composed of ten syllables; the word, which must be chosen not only for its expressive power but also with an eye to its relation to the length of the line; and the individual syllable, which, as will be discussed below, must be placed in a particular rhythmic relationship to every other syllable. Parsing the metre of a Shakespearean poetic line – the process is called 'scansion' – and describing or analysing the effects of metre is easier to do in the classroom than by means of a book. It is both a highly technical activity, where nearly every rule has an exception, and an activity that benefits greatly from reading the poetry aloud and, more importantly, hearing it read aloud by an experienced reader. This chapter, then, can give only the barest of introductions to Shakespeare's metre. It will do so by focusing on the sonnets, which, because they do not need to be located within a larger expository context, provide a more controlled environment for the detailed analysis of metre; the analysis I model can, nevertheless, be applied to most of Shakespeare's dramatic poetry. The aim of the chapter will be to show how Shakespeare writes lines that correspond to the rhythms of ordinary speech, even as they maintain a formal rigour that distinguishes them as poetry. Much as his skill as a dramatist lies in his ability to observe, and yet to treat as permeable, the boundaries between one act or scene and another, so Shakespeare's skill as a poet lies in his ability to work within, and yet to treat as flexible, the poetic conventions he inherited.

In this chapter I will use two sonnets, 129 and 130, to introduce you to, and help you to begin to analyse, Shakespeare's metre. In section A, I use sonnet 130 to describe the metrical foundation of all Shakespeare's pentameter verse. In section B, I use sonnet 129 to demonstrate the extraordinary flexibility of verse built on such a foundation, and I describe some of the poetic effects Shakespeare is able to achieve by putting natural speech rhythms in tension with rigorous poetic form. In section C, I describe and analyse the relation between the two sonnets and suggest that, together, they illuminate Shakespeare's thinking about both the expressive power and the expressive limitations of poetic language.

A.

My mistress' eyes are nothing like the sun;
Coral is far more red than her lips' red;
If snow be white, why then her breasts are dun;
If hairs be wires, black wires grow on her head;
I have seen roses damasked, red and white,
But no such roses see I in her cheeks;
And in some perfumes is there more delight
Than in the breath that from my mistress reeks.
I love to hear her speak, yet well I know
That music hath a far more pleasing sound;
I grant I never saw a goddess go;
My mistress, when she walks, treads on the ground.
And yet, by heaven, I think my love as rare
As any she belied with false compare.

You will probably have heard that Shakespeare's plays and poems are written in 'iambic pentameter'. What does this mean? It means that each line can be measured ('meter') in five ('penta') iambs. An iamb is a pair of syllables – the technical word for this pair is 'foot' – where the first syllable is accented weakly and the second accented strongly. Composed of five iambs, an iambic pentameter line consists of ten syllables. Here is the first line of sonnet 130, where lower-case letters indicate weak accents and capital letters indicate strong:

my MIStress' EYES are NOthing LIKE the SUN

The majority of Shakespeare's lines can be scanned this way. The iambic line is common because it is easy to speak and interesting to hear. It is easy to speak because of the regular alternation between weak and strong accents. It is interesting to hear because most polysyllabic English words are strong on the first syllable and weak on the last (MIStress, NOthing), but the iambic pattern demands that you begin with a weak syllable and end with a strong. Natural rhythms of speech are put in dynamic tension with artificially imposed poetic rhythms.

It would probably be impossible, and in any case uninteresting, to write *only* iambic lines. To accommodate and exploit the natural rhythms of speech, as well as to create rhythmic or musical variety in the poetry, Shakespeare varies the iambic pattern with other kinds of poetic 'feet': the most frequent of these is the 'trochee', which is a pair of syllables arranged STRONG–weak; less frequent though not rare is the 'spondee', which is a pair of syllables arranged STRONG–STRONG. The second line of sonnet 130 begins with a trochee, and finishes with four iambs:

CORal is FAR more RED than HER lips' RED

It is also possible that this line, and line 10, might each contain a spondee; in the quotations below I have put the spondee syllables in boldface as well as capitals.

CORal is FAR **MORE RED** than HER lips' RED

that MUsic HATH a FAR **MORE PLEAS**ing SOUND

Although there are six strong accents if you read the lines this way, the spondee counts, metrically, as only a single beat. I said a moment ago that line 10 'might' contain a spondee: it is important to acknowledge that some ambiguity, and a certain amount of personal judgement, must be a part of most scansion work. It is possible (as I have shown above) to scan line 2 as one trochee plus four iambs, and it is also possible to scan line 10 as completely iambic:

> that MUsic HATH a FAR more PLEAsing SOUND

To my ear, line 2 sounds better without a spondee (perhaps because of the trochee at the beginning), but the sense of line 10 comes across more clearly if 'more' gets an accent as strong as that on 'far' and 'pleasing'. It seems to suit the wry comic tone of the poem to put as much emphasis as possible on the difference between music and the mistress's voice. But the sense probably comes across clearly enough even if you hear 'more' as a weak accent. In this line, poetic form admits a variety of natural speaking approaches.

The interesting thing about sonnet 130 is that except for the first foot of line 2, the fourth foot of line 10 and possibly the third foot of line 2, there is no opportunity, or need, to work against the iambic grain – or to exploit the possibilities of dynamic tension between artificial and natural ways of speaking. In this sonnet, every accent that we might expect to provide the appropriate emphasis in a natural way of speaking corresponds neatly with the metrical demands of its line: 'NOthing' in line 1, 'FAR' in line 2, 'WHITE' and 'DUN' in line 3, 'NO' in line 6, 'MORE' in line 7, 'LOVE' and 'WELL' in line 9, 'YET' in line 13 and 'ANy' in line 14. These are all strongly accented words that fit effortlessly into the iambic pattern; they are also words that help to create the poem's satire on over-used poetic conventions. The poem demonstrates that metre and meaning are inextricably intertwined.

B.

> Th'expense of spirit in a waste of shame
> Is lust in action; and till action, lust
> Is perjured, murd'rous, bloody, full of blame,
> Savage, extreme, rude, cruel, not to trust;
> Enjoyed no sooner but despised straight;
> Past reason hunted, and no sooner had,
> Past reason hated as a swallowed bait,
> On purpose laid to make the taker mad;

Mad in pursuit, and in possession so,
Had, having, and in quest to have, extreme;
A bliss in proof, and proved, a very woe;
Before, a joy proposed; behind, a dream.
All this the world well knows, yet none knows well
To shun the heaven that leads men to this hell.

As in sonnet 130, meaning and metre are inextricably intertwined in sonnet 129, but here the iambic pattern does not correspond effortlessly with the emphases that would occur in a natural way of speaking. Where the metre of sonnet 130 is smooth and regular, the metre of sonnet 129 is rough and conflicted. Lines 1–3 and 5–9 invite a reader to divide them in half, with two strong accents on either side.

th'exPENSE of SPIRit in a WASTE of SHAME

In this line the words 'in a' can be read very quickly. The symmetrical arrangement of the line, with two terms – 'expense, spirit' and 'waste, shame' – on either side of three central weak syllables, encourages a symmetrical, not an alternating, pattern of accent. Line 2 also works this way, with the three weak syllables '-tion; and till' dividing the line in half:

is LUST in ACtion; and till ACtion LUST

The inverted repetition 'lust ... action', 'action lust' also encourages a symmetrical reading. In line 3, the symmetry is created not by the repetition of words across the two halves of the line, but rather by repeated sounds within each half of the line:

is PERjured, MUR'drous, BLOOdy, full of BLAME

'Perjured' and 'mur'drous' have similar vowel sounds, while 'bloody' and 'blame' begin with the same consonant. It should be easy now to see how lines 5 to 9 follow in this pattern: all of them contain four important, strongly accented words (e.g. 'reason hunted' and 'sooner had' in line 6, and 'purpose laid' and 'taker mad' in line 8) separated by three weak accents (e.g. '-er but de-' in line 5 and 'and in po-' in line 9).

Lines 10–14 can, if you read them rapidly, be given the same four-accent pattern I have described in lines 1–3 and 5–9. But it is just as easy, and probably more appropriate, to find a correspondence between the natural way of speaking and full pentameter lines. Line 10's initial spondee seems to demand that a reader slow down; the pattern is iambic thereafter (though it is possible to read spondees in the first and third feet of line 13), with important words occurring on the regularly stressed syllables:

> HAD, HAVing, AND in QUEST to HAVE, exTREME;
>
> a BLISS in PROOF, and PROVED, a VERy WOE,
>
> beFORE, a JOY proPOSED; beHIND, a DREAM.
>
> all THIS the WORLD well KNOWS, yet NONE knows WELL
>
> to SHUN the HEAVEN that LEADS men TO this HELL.

If you read and scan this series of lines slowly and precisely enough to get all five accents in each (where 'heaven' is a monosyllable, pronounced 'heav'n'), and to really feel the pentameter pattern, you will realize that it is possible to read lines 1–3 and 5–9 in the same way. I will demonstrate the pattern of only lines 1 and 5 here, and you can try reading and scanning the rest on your own:

> th'exPENSE of SPIRit IN a WASTE of SHAME
>
> enJOYED no SOONer BUT deSPIsed STRAIGHT

To get all five accents in 1–3 and 5–9, it is necessary both to accent small connecting words ('in', 'but', 'and') that, in a natural way of speaking, are so easy to skim over; and to resist the pull of alliterative patterns in favour of metrical ones (so 'BLOOdy, full of BLAME' in line 3 becomes 'BLOOdy, FULL of BLAME'). To read sonnet 129 is to feel a strong tension, even a conflict, at the structural level (that is, between the first 9 lines and the last 5) and at the level of individual lines, between a more rapid, natural-sounding way of reading where there are four beats to a line and a slower, more artificial-sounding way of reading where there are five.

In the next section, I will discuss some of the implications of the tension in sonnet 129, and make some connections between this tension and the lack of tension in sonnet 130. I want to conclude this section by focusing on the one line in sonnet 129 that I have not yet mentioned: line 4. To read it correctly, you must understand that the word 'cruel' was, in Shakespeare's poetry, almost always pronounced as two syllables (see sonnets 1, 60, 63, 131, 133, 140 and 149) rather than, as is more common in our time, one. Here is how line 4 scans:

SAvage, exTREME, RUDE, CRUel, NOT to TRUST

The line consists of a trochee, an iamb, a spondee and two iambs. The list of adjectives, as well as the rhythm of the preceding three lines, impels you to move through the line at breakneck speed, but you must check your speed in order to navigate the sheer variety of poetic feet, and to give each word, as well as the line as a whole, its full metrical value. The tension between speed and restraint, the complexity of the metrical pattern, and the attention demanded by each syllable in line 4 are exemplary of the challenges presented by the entire poem. Metre and meaning are no less intertwined in sonnet 129 than they are in 130, but in 129 the reader must work much harder to realize the relationship between the two.

C.

Sonnet 129 is about the difficulty of restraining oneself from rushing headlong towards the satisfaction of lustful desires. Everyone knows ('All this the world well knows') that the satisfaction of lust is temporary at best ('a bliss in proof, and proved a very woe'), and that it inevitably leads to regret (is 'despised straight'); but no one can avoid ('shun') the experience because the force of lust is so powerful ('Savage, extreme'). The conflict the poem represents, between licence and restraint, between doing what you want to do and doing what you know you should do, is dramatized not only in the poem's words but also in its metre: in the conflict between a rapid and a restrained way of reading, and between accents that come naturally and accents that are demanded by the metrical conventions that govern sonnet-writing. The very forcefulness of the writing in this sonnet, especially its use of lists, repeated phrases and alliteration, suggests that lust and the conflicted feelings it precipitates are too ferocious to be contained within the boundaries of the poem; at the same time, the metrical arrangement of syllables and words makes a plea for control, even though it is one that a reader might not be able to heed.

Although it sounds very different from, and simpler than, sonnet 129, sonnet 130 dramatizes a similar, and more complex, relation between content and metrical form. Sonnet 130 is about the inadequacy of the conventions of love poetry to the task of representing a lover's feelings truthfully. When poets rely on conventional exaggerations – that a lady's eyes are as bright as the sun, or that her voice is as pleasant as music – they succeed primarily in calling attention to the distance between what they want to describe and the thing they have used to describe it. These 'false' comparisons are a form of lying about the beloved that might easily be contradicted by plain, direct speech: 'And yet I think my love more fair ...'. Like its digest of love-poem imagery (sun, coral, snow, roses, perfume, music, goddess), the sonnet's metrical regularity is a convention that Shakespeare uses against the sonnet itself: the very simplicity of the poem, not only in its metre but in its rigorous confinement of comparisons to single lines and pairs of lines, is an exaggeration or parody of love poetry that is no more than the sum of its own devices. At the same time, as I have argued in section A of this chapter, the metrical regularity of the sonnet is also part of its persuasive force. Moreover, the poem, in anatomizing and critiquing the conventions of bad love poetry, makes a paradoxical claim for itself *as* a love poem: the best kind of love poetry, it seems to say, is love poetry that understands that the conventions of love poetry are deceptive. As sonnet 129's metrical complexity dramatizes the conflict in the poem between desire and restraint discussed in the poem, so sonnet 130's metrical simplicity dramatizes the poem's conflicted view of the extent to which any love poem can represent love truthfully.

Conclusion

As with so many things in Shakespeare, we cannot be certain whether the order of his 154 sonnets, printed for the first time in 1609 but undoubtedly circulated privately (in part or in their entirety) more than a decade earlier, is the order he intended for them or an order imposed by the printer. There is no discernible overarching narrative sequence to the sonnets, but many pairs, trios and larger groups of them (for example 1–17, 29 and 30, 33 and 34, 89 and 90, and 109–11) are clearly meant to be understood *as* groups. If sonnets 129 and 130 were not intended to be printed side by side, it is a very lucky accident that they were. Each sonnet approaches a related problem – the inadequacy of poetic conventions to the task of expressing an intense feeling – from a different direction, and the two poems side by side vividly demonstrate the dazzling range of sonic, tonal and metrical effects Shakespeare was able to achieve within rigorous formal constraints.

CHAPTER FOURTEEN

Textual Variation

Overview

Many of Shakespeare's plays were printed in multiple versions during his lifetime, and there are often numerous and significant differences between the versions of any given play. To take an example already discussed (see section C of Chapter Eleven), Richard II's speech about the 'king of snow' (4.1.254) did not appear in the earliest printed text (1597) of that play. Indeed, the entire scene in which Bolingbroke tries to persuade Richard to resign the crown – which includes not only the snow-king speech, but also Richard's metaphor of the two buckets (4.1.182–9), his ritualistic self-divestment (4.1.201–22) and his shattering of the mirror (4.1.273–91) – does not appear in the 1597 edition. We do not know whether this scene was censored in print but performed on the stage, or censored both in print and on the stage, or simply not written when *Richard II* had its premiere *c.* 1596; and, therefore, we do not know whether the 1608 text of the play, which does contain the scene (as do all subsequent editions), is an augmented or a restored version of the original. All we know for certain is that the two texts are variant, and that a version of *Richard II* without all the dense, thematically resonant material from 4.1 would be a very different play from the version most of us will read, study and see performed. What is the nature of that difference, and to what extent can we perceive, through that difference, Shakespeare's process of composition and revision – as well as the establishment of a critical and editorial tradition that represents Shakespeare in a particular way? These are the kinds of questions you can begin to ask and answer when you bring to your analysis of Shakespeare's poetic language an awareness of textual variation.

Your edition of *Richard II* is almost certainly based on a text printed in 1608 or later and so contains the 'complete' version of 4.1. Many editions provide a footnote pointing out that some of the scene's lines were not in the play's earliest text, and most editions mention the play's textual history in their introductions. In either case, it is likely that you could read *Richard II* without ever suspecting that the text you are reading has been deliberately chosen from among a couple of alternatives, or that one of its most important scenes might be a variation – introduced on the occasion of a repeat printing and expanding the scene's meaning – rather than what Shakespeare originally wrote. The fact that you can read the play without being aware of its complex textual history is not necessarily a problem in the case of *Richard II* – I think the play would be worse, and less interesting to read or study, with the shorter version of 4.1. But an awareness of the textual history can enrich your understanding of the play and help you become conscious of how your own interpretations of character and action are constructed by which words are and are not on the page. In the case of some plays (*Hamlet* is the most famous example), an awareness of textual history is essential to understanding the interpretive problems raised by Shakespeare's language.

There is not space in this short book to explain how variant texts of Shakespeare's plays came to be produced in the sixteenth and seventeenth centuries, or the conventions by which critics and editors have adjudicated their relative reliability. A good teacher, or the introduction to a good modern edition, should be able to give you an overview of these matters, and direct you to some useful critical readings. In this chapter I discuss some well-known examples of textual variation and model some ways of analysing them, and of using them to analyse the plays of which they are a part. The first example, from *A Midsummer Night's Dream* (section A), is a common type of textual variation that invites and rewards interpretation: lines assigned to one character in one version of the play are assigned to another in another. The second example, from *King Lear* (section B), is also a common type of textual variation:

a single word changes from one version of the text to another, and the change significantly affects the meaning of the passage. Both these examples make it clear that Shakespeare's plays underwent multiple stages, or perhaps a continuous process, of writing and revision, before and after they were first performed. The chapter's final example (section C) discusses a duplicated passage assigned to two different characters in one of the texts of *Romeo and Juliet*, and suggests that it is possible to think in aesthetic terms even about variations that are the result of errors in printing.

A.

A Midsummer Night's Dream, probably first performed around 1595, was printed for the first time in 1600. It was then reprinted in the Folio edition of Shakespeare's plays compiled after the playwright's death and published in 1623. The two texts are mostly consistent with one another. One exception, which I shall discuss here, has to do with the men who serve Duke Theseus. In both versions of the text, Theseus speaks, in the play's first scene, to a character named Philostrate, ordering him to 'Stir up the Athenian youth to merriments' (1.1.12) in advance of the duke's wedding to Hippolyta. No sooner has Philostrate left the stage to do Theseus's bidding than Egeus, Hermia's father, enters to complain about his daughter's love for the wrong man. After listening to his complaint, Theseus orders Hermia, on pain of death, to marry Demetrius. The plot unfolds from here, arriving at its comic climax at the end of Act 4, when Egeus, Theseus and Hippolyta – out for a hunt on the morning of the wedding – find the lovers asleep in the forest. The duke, obviously in a festive mood, announces that he will 'overbear' Egeus's will and then invites Hermia and Lysander, Helena and Demetrius to be married alongside himself and Hippolyta 'in the Temple'.

In the 1600 text of the play, this is the last we see of Egeus. Shylock-like, he disappears after a duke turns against his plea for 'law' (4.1.154) and he loses control of his daughter. In the 1623 text, however, Egeus is directed to enter with Theseus and Hippolyta at the beginning of Act 5. Not only that, but he then serves as the master of ceremonies for the wedding revels: 'Say what abridgement have you for this evening,' Theseus asks him, 'What masque? What music?' As Egeus prepares to read from a 'brief' that lists the 'many sports' available, the list seems to be snatched from his hand by Lysander, who reads out most of the options to Theseus (with Theseus rejecting each in turn) before Egeus takes over again and describes the Mechanicals' production of *Pyramus and Thisbe*. This is quite a different scene from the one given in the 1600 text, where Philostrate hands Theseus the 'brief', which Theseus then reads aloud himself, commenting upon it as he goes. The 1600 text, then, represents the total suppression of Egeus: the father's will is no match for the play's drive towards a comic resolution, and we can assume that Hermia thinks as little about Egeus as we do once he is gone. The 1623 text takes a more realistic approach, and in doing so might insist upon the costs of a comic resolution: Egeus, as a noble servant of the duke, is not allowed to miss the wedding. Not only must he attend and see his daughter married against his wishes, but he must be the one responsible for stirring up mirth, and he must suffer the humiliation of Lysander's taunts. Hermia, meanwhile, can hardly pretend that her father doesn't exist – or, if she can, then it is something that we must almost certainly notice.

Your modern edition probably follows the 1600 text – most editions do, though there is at least one good, modern classroom edition (Oxford, 1994, edited by Peter Holland) that follows the 1623. The chief argument against the 1623 text is that it is illogical: if Egeus is to serve as master of the revels in the final scene, why does Shakespeare trouble to name a silent character, Philostrate, in the first scene and assign him this function? Why would Egeus perform this function but not speak lines that explicitly showed that he was reconciled (or not) to his daughter's wedding? Why would Theseus allow Lysander to interfere with the ceremonial festivities (everyone knows wedding festivities must be carefully choreographed) – and why would Lysander presume to do so? Valid as they are, these questions cannot obscure the fact that the 1623 version of the scene is not simply a mistake, the accidental substitution of one speech-prefix for another due to a printer's error or an unclear manuscript. The 1623 version of the scene is a different scene altogether, with a theatrical logic of its own; it is an indication that, in respect of his dramatic material, Shakespeare was willing to allow one thing to turn into another. If you read the 1623 scene closely, it might change the way you read, and understand the theatrical logic of, other parts of the play. In the first scene, for example, after Theseus has heard Egeus's complaint and warned Helena to obey her father, he says to Demetrius and Egeus: 'go along: / I must employ you in some business / Against our nuptial, and confer with you / Of something nearly that concerns yourselves' (1.1.123–6). He never says more specifically what it is he wants to talk about. Maybe it's the wedding entertainment.

B.

How do you go about finding textual variation that might expand and enrich your experience of a Shakespeare play? Modern editions, especially those aimed at students, tend to strive above all for clarity, and are reluctant to involve readers in the problems posed by a scene like *Dream* 5.1. Matters of textual history and variation are by and large dealt with in a literally marginal way: especially if there is extensive variation between texts, an editor's introduction will provide explanatory narratives for the state of the texts; and local variations will generally be recorded at the bottom of each page – either in footnotes or, in some editions, the textual notes at the bottom of each page. The textual notes provide a genealogical record of the text's origins and allow an editor to show his or her work: if the modern edition prints a word that is substantively different from the word that appears in an early text, the word as it appears in the early text – and often in previous modern editions – will be given in the textual notes. Sometimes a modern editor's choice of a word will have a complicated enough relation to what is recorded in the textual notes to warrant discussion in a separate footnote. These footnotes are usually clear indicators of an opportunity for rewarding close reading. A classic example is *Hamlet* 1.2.129, where editors remain undecided whether Hamlet refers to his 'flesh' as 'too too sallied' (1603 and 1604 texts), 'too too solid' (1623 text) or 'too too sullied' (a conjecture of many editors since the eighteenth century).

If you are interested in the kind of close reading enabled by an awareness of textual variation, it is worth looking even at uncontroversial variants in the textual notes. Here are two famous lines from the 1623 text of *King Lear*, which you will find in almost every modern edition of that play. They are spoken by the recently blinded Gloucester, just as he begins to contemplate a suicidal leap from what he believes to be the cliffs of Dover.

> As flies to wanton boys, are we to the gods.
> They kill us for their sport.
>
> (4.1.38–9)

It is a vividly bleak sentiment and absolutely appropriate to both the immediate context and the play as a whole: everyone in *Lear* lives under the threat of a sudden, arbitrary, violent catastrophe. We might well see the play's world as one overseen by frivolous and malicious gods.

If you look at the textual notes on the page where these lines occur in the most recent Arden edition of *Lear*, you will see the following series of disconnected numbers, words, and abbreviations:

> 38 to wanton] *F*; are toth'wanton *Q* 39 kill] *F*; bitt *Q*

What does it all mean? Each number refers to a line, and each bracketed word or phrase to a word or phrase as it appears in the modern edition. Immediately after the bracket is the text from which the editor has drawn his reading – the 1623 Folio printing of Shakespeare's works (*F*) in each case here. After the semicolon are given alternative readings, usually from other early printings: in the 1608 Quarto (*Q*) 'flies to wanton' appeared as 'flies are toth'wanton'; and 'kill' as 'bitt'. These textual notes provide a glimpse of the internal anatomy of the modern edition – of all the choices, small and large, an editor must make from a long and complicated editorial tradition in order to present you, the reader, with a legible text.

To demonstrate how the textual notes might be put to work by the close reader, I will now unfold them into a quotation of the two lines as they appear in the 1608 text:

> As flies are to th' wanton boys, are we to th' gods,
> They bitt us for their sport.

It is just possible that 'bitt' is a misprint for 'kill', but it is more likely that it is an irregular spelling of 'bite'. These lines are not quite as elegant as the 1623 version, where the two halves of the first line are kept neatly parallel: 'flies' goes with 'we' and 'wanton boys' goes with 'gods'. These parallels are made clear by the verb of the second line, 'They kill': that is, wanton boys 'kill' flies. In the 1608 text, the two halves are twisted rather than parallel: because the verb in the second line is 'bitt' (something flies might do to boys), 'flies' in the first line must go with 'gods' and 'boys' with 'we'. Not only is this less elegant than the 1623 version, it is also much less bleak, diminishing both men and gods: Gloucester here does not conceive of humanity as doomed to be the helpless victims of sadistic divinities, but rather as plagued by gods no more irritating than flies.

The sentiment is unusual, and perhaps not exactly what we would expect from a man who has recently had his eyes gouged out; nor is it as satisfying a representation of the total experience of *Lear* as you get from the lines in the 1623 text. That is, the image of biting flies and mischievous boys is out of proportion to the magnitude of the suffering endured and inflicted by the characters in the play. But if you accept the image as authorial in origin (that is, not just a printer's error) you might be able to reread the play with a sense that its solemn tragedy is shaped, or sharpened, by grim comedy. Perhaps the most nihilistic thing about the play is that it makes all suffering seem equal – equally meaningless, equally a tedious inevitability (like the biting of flies) to be got through as best you can, equally endured by men and women who are as petty and self-involved as mischievous children. 'Great thing of us forgot!' the reformed Albany says (5.3.235) when he realizes that Lear and Cordelia are still in prison and in danger of execution. *Forgot*! What a stupid mistake precipitates the play's ultimate tragedy! And the action that follows upon this, where Albany first tries to give over 'absolute power' to Lear (299, an obvious mistake) and then, after Lear dies, to divide the kingdom between Edgar and Kent (318–19, a repetition of Lear's initial mistake), gives little hope that this is the last or even the worst tragedy that England will face. Tragedies will continue to plague men, like flies.

C.

Two versions of *Romeo and Juliet* were printed during Shakespeare's lifetime, one in 1597 and one in 1599. Most modern editions are based on the 1599 edition, which is generally considered a more reliable text in its representation of Shakespeare's intentions, or of what the play looked like in its early performances, or both. One element of the 1599 text that is probably not visible in your modern edition, however, is the fact that it preserves two slightly different versions of the same passage – and assigns each to a different speaker – in the transition between 2.2 (the 'balcony scene') and 2.3 (the first entrance of the friar). This is different from the 1597 text, which contains only one version of the passage and assigns it to the friar alone. I have modernized the spelling in the following quotation, and, for clarity's sake, put the repeated passage in boldface.

> *Romeo.* Would I were sleep and peace so sweet to rest.
> **The grey eyed morn smiles on the frowning night,**
> **Check'ring the eastern clouds with streaks of light,**
> **And darkness fleckted like a drunkard reels,**
> **From forth day's pathway, made by Titan's wheels.**
> Hence will I to my ghostly Friar's close cell,
> His help to crave, and my dear hap to tell. *Exit.*
>
> *Enter Friar alone with a basket.*
>
> *Friar.* **The grey-eyed morn smiles on the frowning night,**
> **Checking the eastern clouds with streaks of light:**
> **And fleckled darkness like a drunkard reels,**
> **From forth day's path, and Titan's burning wheels.**
> Now ere the sun advance his burning eye,
> The day to cheer, and night's dank dew to dry ...

It is likely that Shakespeare wrote both versions of the passage, and that only one of them was meant to be spoken on the stage; and it is possible, but by no means certain, that one of the passages was marked for deletion in the manuscript from which the edition was printed. The preservation of both versions in the printed text is clearly an error, but since no manuscript text of *Romeo and Juliet* (or any other Shakespeare play) is extant, the origins of the error cannot be determined and a correction cannot easily be decided upon. It is the job of the modern editor to decide upon and justify the correct version of this passage, and most readers will probably not suffer from being unaware that a decision has been made. If, however, you, the close reader, discover the variation through research or come across it in the textual notes or the footnotes, it is productive to consider whether anything can be done with it in critical terms.

As so often, the most important point here is also the simplest: in writing out two slightly different versions of the passage, imagining both Romeo and the friar speaking it, Shakespeare clearly felt that this evocation of night turning into dawn was important. He liked what he had written and wanted to be sure to get it into the play, even though he wasn't sure how it would fit. We must not allow the presence of a textual error (whether originating with the printer or with the manuscript he was printing from) to obscure the fact that Shakespeare imagines the passage to be doing vital work for the play. We must next acknowledge that the work the passage does in the play is, in typical Shakespearean fashion, excessive. Whether spoken by the friar, whom we have never seen before, or by Romeo, whose language to this point has seldom strayed beyond the self-regarding conventions of love poetry, this passage marks a real change in the play's idiom: this is the language of epic poetry, not of a modern, urban love story.

If we imagine that Romeo is meant to speak the passage, we might say that his love for Juliet and the energy of his encounter with her has elevated him: he suddenly speaks a new language. If we imagine that the speaker must be the friar, we might say that this is Shakespeare's way of using a peripheral character to provide, unwittingly, a poetic perspective that gives to a rather ordinary conflict (teenagers in love disobeying their parents) an epic dimension. In either case, Shakespeare has decided that what is necessary in the moment after Romeo and Juliet's fate-sealing secret rendezvous is a passage that concentrates, in grandiose poetic language, the imagery of dark and light, day and night, which saturates the play. Out of a rather prosaic romantic conflict erupts poetic art in the high style.

Conclusion

Textual variation in *Romeo and Juliet* (1599) Act 2 is excessive in itself: there are more lines and more speakers then we need. I have suggested, here and throughout the book, that the best thing to do is read that excess for itself, rather than decide which part of it to cut away. This is not to say that Shakespeare might not have preferred to attribute the speech to one character rather than another; nor is it to say that an interpretation of *Romeo and Juliet* is impoverished if it is based on a modern edition that makes only one alternative available. Rather, it is to say that textual history – the repetition and variation that occur as texts are produced and reproduced over time – viewed under the lens of close reading, is a constitutive element of a play's meaning. One further example, from *Richard III*, will serve to demonstrate this point and to summarize some of the main ideas and methods of this book.

> What do I fear? my self? there's none else by,
> Richard loves Richard, that is I and I.

It is the night before the battle of Bosworth Field. Richard III has just awakened from a nightmare in which he was visited by the ghosts of those he has killed. Each ghost foretells his doom and promises Richmond success. The two lines quoted come at the beginning of a long speech in which Richard works himself up into a state of despair about his history of violence and his future damnation. What begins as an attempt to take comfort in his solitude after his rather crowded dream – 'there's none else by' – quickly gives way to an expression of split identity: loving himself, alone with himself, Richard is two *I*s. Or, at least, that is the reading of the 1597 text of *Richard III*. All later printings of the play, including the 1623 text, contain a crucial variation, where Richard attempts, through self-love, to reaffirm his singularity:

> What? do I fear my self? There's none else by,
> Richard loves Richard, that is, I am I.

'I and I' or 'I am I': the phrases are at once nearly identical and sharply distinct. It is just possible that the variation is the result of a corrected printer's error (that is, where the later printings correct the 1597 text), but it is more interesting, and entirely plausible, to imagine that the variation records Shakespeare's productive uncertainty about how to express what Richard feels.

We will never know which text is the 'correct' one: we will always have both, and arguments in favour of one or the other must always, finally, be a matter of interpretation. In both texts,

Richard's sense of tumultuous inner division is closely connected to a feeling of loneliness. Following the logic of the premise introduced by repeating his own name, he is gradually forced to admit that he has more reason to hate than to love himself: conscience, 'with a thousand several tongues' (194), condemns him as a villain and makes him realize that there 'is no creature loves me, / And if I die, no soul will pity me' (201–2). The oscillation between 'I and I' and 'I am I' in the passage with which I began expresses something in textual terms which is true of the speech in thematic terms: Richard's terror, and the extraordinary theatrical energy of this moment, lies in the paradox that, in his very singularity, he is divided against himself.

Shakespeare's poetic language is characterized by excess: it almost always contains more than it is possible to comprehend in a single reading. Good close reading attempts to do justice to the excess of Shakespeare's language by describing it as fully as possible, and such reading attempts to make that excess intelligible by focusing on those moments in which it generates multiple perspectives on a play's main ideas. An awareness of textual variation allows the close reader to see that excess was a constitutive element of Shakespeare's process of composition – indeed, that it was a result of his willingness to revise or rethink or leave open the meanings and possible meanings of any given word, image, speech or action. In his astonishing capacity for poetic invention, Shakespeare was often, like many of his own characters, divided against himself.

EPILOGUE

> Glory is like a circle in the water,
> Which never ceaseth to enlarge itself
> Till by broad spreading it disperse to nought.
>
> (*1 Henry VI* 1.2.133–5)

The passage above is one of my favorite things in all of Shakespeare. Its movement from 'glory' to 'nought' seems to trace the circular shape it describes. The image is at once concrete and ephemeral: almost as soon as you begin to envision the circle, you must begin to envision its disappearance. But that disappearance is of a particular kind. A circle in the water does not vanish; rather, it becomes indistinguishable from the water's surface. Like so many examples in this book, the passage represents the energetic moment at which one thing turns into another, simultaneously losing and becoming more like itself. I present it, by way of conclusion, as exemplary of the kind of passage that most inspires my own close reading and as a figure for the work of close reading itself.

From this book's title, to its textbook-style chapter format, to its language of 'modelling' and 'demonstration', it has implied an objectivity of method and result that many readers may find at odds with their assumptions about critical and imaginative engagement with literature. Surely a textbook method of literary analysis, however rigorously applied, will produce different results from one reader to the next, because of the different experiences, priorities and frames of reference each reader brings to the text. And surely, to the extent that the method provided could produce replicable results, it would fail to capture what is most exciting and interesting about a critical and imaginative engagement with literature, namely the freedom of interpretation – the freedom both to listen to and to speak back to the text. Both things are true.

I have intended this book to be *useful* to readers insofar as it identifies productive sites for analysis and interpretation, and addresses some fundamental questions about the relation between part and whole in the experience of Shakespeare's poetic language. But I expect that in the moments where the book is most *successful*, my analysis and interpretation say something about a play that seems true and that you did not see before. In these moments, I hope, my close reading of the play makes reading closely seem both possible and worthwhile, and inspires you to undertake the task on your own terms.

Shakespeare's language rewards close reading, but that reading can take many forms and admit any number of interpretations. Perhaps the most rewarding thing about the process of close reading is being able to return to the plays and poems over and over, finding new things in them, new ways of seeing and hearing them, each time. The next most rewarding thing is being able to share what you have seen and heard with another reader, and so to make your observations a part of the ongoing life of the text. This is also the most difficult thing, for as much as Shakespeare's language might seem to provide a 'common ground' for all readers, its extraordinary multiplicity makes it more like the surface of a pond – fluid, glittering, yielding a different view of its depths and its shallows depending on the position of the observer, the quality of the light and the weather of the moment. We might imagine that the goal of close reading and analysis is to create a ripple on that pond: a refined, fleeting shape on an unstable surface, the record of an energetic engagement with the text which is now a part of the whole that has assimilated it.

SELECTED FURTHER READING

As I said in the Preface, this book should not be mistaken for, or used as, a course in Shakespeare studies. If you are interested in reading more about Shakespeare, his plays, and the theatrical, social and political milieu in which he wrote them, or if you are interested in beginning to discover the vast range of critical and theoretical approaches to his plays, you should consult the instructor of any Shakespeare course you are taking, the bibliographies in modern editions of the plays, and a good library catalogue. Here I have given a very select list of works that provide examples of close reading that are similar to or have been influential for the kind of close reading I have modelled in this book. Not all of them are exclusively concerned with Shakespeare; all of them will provide you with useful tools for, and expand your understanding of what is exciting about, reading Shakespeare's language closely.

Sylvia Adamson, Lynette Hunter and Lynne Magnusson, eds, *Reading Shakespeare's Dramatic Language: A Guide* (London: Arden Shakespeare, 2001)

Harry Berger, Jr., *Imaginary Audition: Shakespeare on Page and Stage* (Berkeley: University of California Press, 1989)

David Bevington, *Action is Eloquence: Shakespeare's Language of Gesture* (Cambridge, MA: Harvard University Press, 1984)

Stephen Booth, 'On the Value of *Hamlet*', in Norman Rabkin, ed., *Reinterpretations of Elizabethan Drama* (New York: Columbia University Press, 1969), 137–76

Cleanth Brooks, *The Well Wrought Urn: Studies in the Structure of Poetry* (New York: Reynal & Hitchcock, 1947)

Reuben Brower, *The Fields of Light: An Experiment in Critical Reading* (Oxford: Oxford University Press, 1951)

Maurice Charney, *How to Read Shakespeare* (New York: Peter Lang, 1992)

Alan Dessen, *Elizabethan Stage Conventions and Modern Interpreters* (Cambridge: Cambridge University Press, 1984)

Madeleine Doran, *Shakespeare's Dramatic Language: Essays* (Madison: University of Wisconsin Press, 1976)

William Empson, *Seven Types of Ambiguity* (London: Chatto & Windus, 1953)

Jean Howard, *Shakespeare's Art of Orchestration: Stage Technique and Audience Response* (Urbana: University of Illinois Press, 1984)

Russ McDonald, *Shakespeare and the Arts of Language* (Oxford: Oxford University Press, 2001)

Russ McDonald, Nicholas Nace and Travis Williams, eds, *Shakespeare Up Close: Reading Early Modern Texts* (London: Arden Shakespeare, 2012)

Simon Palfrey and Tiffany Stern, *Shakespeare in Parts* (Oxford: Oxford University Press, 2007)

Caroline Spurgeon, *Shakespeare's Imagery and What it Tells Us* (Cambridge: Cambridge University Press, 1936)

Gary Taylor, *Moment by Moment by Shakespeare* (Newark: University of Delaware Press, 1985)

George T. Wright, *Shakespeare's Metrical Art* (Berkeley: University of California Press, 1988)

Paul Yachnin, *Shakespeare's World of Words* (London: Bloomsbury, 2015)

INDEX

All's Well That Ends Well 4, 5, 59–61, 72–3, 95–7, 113, 116–20, 122
Antony and Cleopatra 33–6, 38, 59, 75, 103–4, 105
As You Like It 5, 104–6

Comedy of Errors, The 3–4, 5, 68–9, 78, 125, 132–7
Coriolanus 12, 24, 64, 70, 98, 102
Cymbeline 6–7, 76–7

Hamlet 10, 20, 33–7, 38, 76, 78, 110, 125–7, 128, 151, 154
Henry IV, Part 1 6, 8, 41–51, 61, 76, 83, 86, 102, 123
Henry IV, Part 2 6, 8, 83
Henry V 31–3, 80, 82–6, 89, 97–8
Henry VI, Part 1 161
Henry VI, Part 2 8
Henry VI, Part 3 79

Julius Caesar 6, 8, 20, 37, 56–7, 58, 59, 129–32

King John 6
King Lear 8–9, 68, 76, 78, 106, 151–2, 154–6

Love's Labour's Lost 5

Macbeth 59, 61–2, 68, 101, 109–10, 113–16, 122, 128–9, 134
Measure for Measure 5, 62–3, 66, 76
Merchant of Venice, The 22–3, 59, 65–6, 67, 70, 106–7
Merry Wives of Windsor, The 76
Midsummer Night's Dream, A 5, 37–9, 59, 70, 76, 91–3, 97, 151–4
Much Ado About Nothing 5, 10, 61

Othello 10, 18, 28, 31, 32–3, 64, 68, 70, 74–5, 77, 98, 102–3, 105, 109, 124

Pericles 6

Richard II 61, 67–8, 70, 77–8, 106, 113, 120–2, 150–1
Richard III 61, 79, 109–10, 159–60
Romeo and Juliet 59, 68, 70, 78, 98–100, 108–9, 123, 125, 153, 156–9

Sonnets 141–9

Taming of the Shrew, The 4–5, 12–16, 55–6, 58, 59, 80–2, 88, 89
Tempest, The 28–31, 32–3
Titus Andronicus 6, 17–22, 80, 86–9, 93–5, 107–8
Troilus and Cressida 39–40, 66–7, 75–6, 137–8
Twelfth Night 5, 23–4, 61
Two Gentlemen of Verona, The 5, 96–7

Winter's Tale, The 24–5, 58–9, 73–4, 75, 107–8